THE FALL OF FRANCE

Act with Daring

Actions speak louder than words. In the days to come the
Goddess of Victory will bestow her laurels only on those who
are prepared to act with daring.

Heinz Guderian, 1937.

THE FALL OF FRANCE

Act with Daring

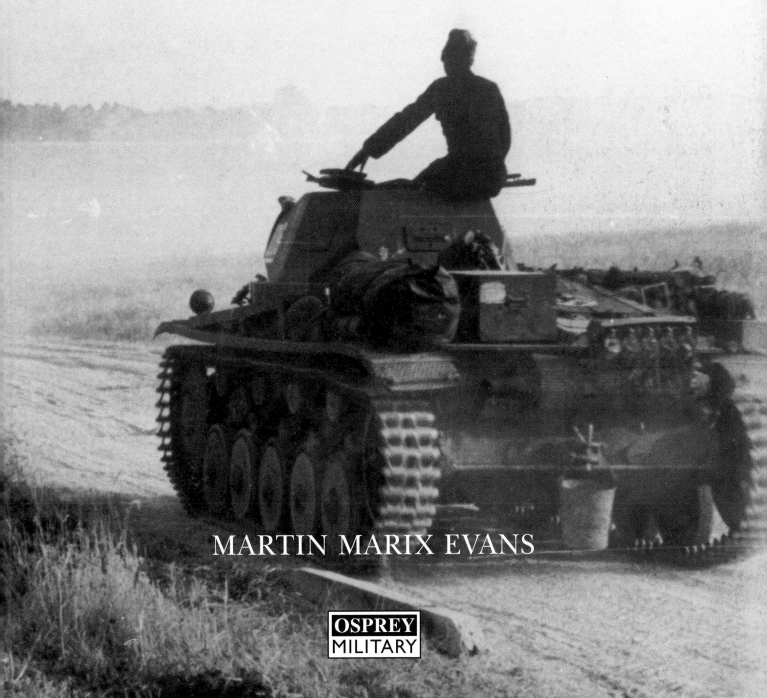

MARTIN MARIX EVANS

OSPREY
MILITARY

First published in Great Britain in 2000 by Osprey Publishing,
Elms Court, Chapel Way, Botley, Oxford OX2 9LP, UK
E-mail: info@ospreypublishing.com

ISBN 1 85532 969 7

Editor: Marcus Cowper
Layout by: Ken Vail Graphic Design
Origination by Valhaven, Isleworth, UK
Printed in China through World Print Ltd

00 01 02 03 04   10 9 8 7 6 5 4 3 2 1

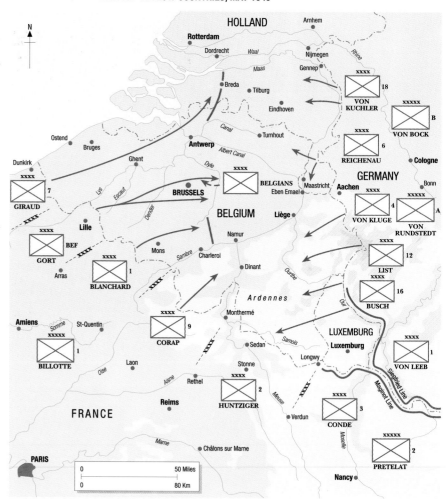

THE INVASION OF FRANCE AND THE LOW COUNTRIES, MAY 1940

ACKNOWLEDGEMENTS

For their help in making some inroads in my ignorance of what happened where
in Belgium I must thank Michael Baert of the Belgian Tourist Office, Brussels
and Ardennes, in London, Pierre Gosset, former secretary to C.R.I.B.A. in
Belgium and Guy Blockmans in Brussels and Patrice Legros in Liège. Mr H.
Lardinois of the Institut Géographique National in Brussels directed me to
contemporary mapping. I thank Andrew Saunders for his help in introducing me
to Robert Gils of Simon Stevinstchting, and to Mr Gils for his help in giving me
what modest understanding of the Belgian fortresses I now possess as well as
guiding me to appropriate maps. Captain David Horn of the Guards Museum
in London, Richard Callaghan of the Royal Sussex Regiment Museum and
Alan Readman of the West Sussex Record Office gave valuable advice and
introductions. Mrs P. James and Roy Harding of the Queen's Royal Surrey
Regiment Museum were very helpful to me. David Fletcher and his colleagues at
the Tank Museum, Bovington, were unfailing in their kindness. Peter Liddle and
Claire Harder of the Second World War Experience Centre produced some
fascinating material for me, in spite of having been operational for only a
matter of weeks. In the Netherlands Wybo Boersma gave me guidance and my
sister, Amina Marix Evans, undertook research for me and discovered valuable
information about the events of May 1940.

I have relied to a considerable extent on the memoirs of Heinz Guderian and
Erwin Rommel as published in English translations in the preparation of this
book. Those sources, and the sources of many other quotations by individuals are
from their published works, listed in detail in the bibliography. I am extremely
grateful to the Second World War Experience Centre for the information on the
experience of T. G. P. Crick and the quotations from C. N. Barker and W.
Marett. The Queens Royal Surrey Regimental Museum is the source of the
memoirs of Stanley Rayner, John Redfern and John Naylor. I am particularly
grateful to Douglas Swift who has allowed me to quote from his unpublished

memoir of the action at Amiens and has also provided a sketch of his battalion's
dispositions. I am indebted to the Hon. Caroline Ponsonby for being allowed to
quote from the papers of her father, Major Lord Sysonby. I have also had the
good fortune to be given a first-hand account of his experiences as an anti-aircraft
gunner by Albert Smith. At the time of going to press the owners of certain copy-
rights have not been traced and I would be grateful for information as to their
identity and whereabouts.

The maps used are mostly those published in Berlin by the army in preparation
for the invasion of France and the Low Countries or German maps made later in
the war showing useful detail of important locations. Some come from my own
collection while the rest are from the Bodleian Library, Oxford, and carry the
annotation 'BL' and the appropriate shelf number. Permission to reproduce maps
from the Bodleian Library is gratefully acknowledged and, even more important
to me, the patience and helpfulness of the staff of the Map Room deserves high
praise. The British maps are from a private collection and I am grateful for the
grant of access. Ordnance Survey maps are Crown Copyright.

The photographs from the Bundesarchiv in Koblenz are annotated with the letter B
and the reference number of the image, while those from the Imperial War Museum
are marked IWM and those from the Tank Museum TM, with their reference
numbers. I am grateful for permission to reproduce these pictures and for the assistance
given to me in my research at these archives. I am also grateful for being allowed to
use illustrations from private collections, some of which were taken by the owners
themselves. In the Netherlands Mr Wybo Boersma of the Airborne Museum,
Hartenstein, Mr G. Koenen, Mr A. C. Duijvestijn and the Dutch Marines have been
most kind in this respect. Bart van Bulck, Franck Vernier and David Playne have
contributed photographs of installations in Belgium. Amina Marix Evans has
contributed to the modern colour photographs, most of which are my own.
Attributions are included in the captions.

CONTENTS

MAPS AND PLANS

Place and date of publication given where possible. German 1:25,000 mapping made in France during the occupation is annotated GM, and was not available to them in 1940.

THE PHONEY WAR

When Britain finally went to war alongside France against Germany on 3 September 1939, it was with the confidence that her own lack of sufficient, trained troops would be compensated for by the might of the French army. The five divisions available for the British Expeditionary Force (BEF) would be followed by a further five and take their place in the line with a much greater number of French divisions. As Winston Churchill was to remark, 'Thank God for the French army!'

The serious preparations for war had begun only some six months earlier. It was then thought that France would be able to mobilise 72 divisions to add to the fortress troops which numbered some 12 divisions. The Germans, it was estimated, would be in a position to put 116 divisions in the field, but because they would have to conquer Poland before attacking France, that number would be somewhat depleted

when the time came. As far as air power was concerned, it was calculated the Allies had about 850 each of fighters and bombers and some 950 reconnaissance and army co-operation aircraft against 1,000 fighters, nearly twice as many bombers and about 800 reconnaissance and army co-operation aircraft. There appears to have been little, if any, discussion of armoured fighting vehicles (AFVs) – tanks, armoured cars and armoured troop carriers.

The battlefield, it was assumed, would be on the French borders. The east, facing Germany, was already equipped with the most sophisticated and secure complex of fortresses Europe had ever seen, the Maginot Line. Within a steel and concrete carapace, for the most part buried underground and with artillery-bearing turrets commanding the approaches, hundreds of men could eat, sleep, relax, exercise and stand guard to preserve the integrity of French soil.

André Maurois wrote;

'What has already, before the supreme test, deserved all the wonder and praise is the fact alone that generals and engineers have dared to convert into fortresses not only whole mountains, but a whole range of mountains, that they should have impregnated with fire every inch of the threatened ground all along our north-eastern frontiers and found Government after Government willing to give them the necessary millions ... The English never wearied of poring over the annotated photographs, the firing-maps, the drawings and the diagrams which mean that on a single telephone call of three or four figures, a storm of shells will rain on such and such a segment of wood B17, or such and such a section of territory 243. They were fascinated by the perfection of detail ...'

Between these strongholds, to avoid their being outflanked and by-passed as they had been in the First World War, mobile interval troops supported the static works. This impressive, expensive and ultimately futile defence ran from the Swiss border to La Ferté, 24km (15 miles) south-east of Sedan. The 35 divisions of General G. Prételat's Army Group 2, a third of the French army, held that line. To the west of the last fort a string of strongpoints, concrete bunkers and pill-boxes, straggled along the Meuse and across northern France towards Lille where it petered out, partly because of insufficient funds, partly to avoid disrupting a region of immense industrial and commercial importance and partly to avoid excluding the Belgians, allies in the last war and probable allies in the next.

When Maurois's book, *The Battle of France*, was later published he added a footnote to his chapter on the Maginot Line, saying:

'We know now that the Maginot line-complex was a dangerous disease of the mind; but I publish this as it was written in January, 1940.'

In November 1939 the South African High Commissioner to London, Deneys Reitz, visited France. Reitz had fought his first war 40 years earlier, against the British in the Second Anglo-Boer War. His second had been not for, but, as he explained, with the British against the Germans, when he rose to the command of the 1st Royal Scots Fusiliers. Now, the representative of his country, he toured familiar territory making ready for yet another war. He was not much impressed. He reports a conversation with Gamelin who complained bitterly of the lack of Belgian co-operation in making the Maginot Line complete and their continued obstinacy in refusing staff liaison in the face of the German threat. He viewed the line under construction by the British east of Lille.

'We shook our heads at what we saw. The new line, under hurried construction, seemed an amateurish affair. The trenches were shallow, the concrete domes the French had built at intervals of eight hundred yards [730m.] contained only a single anti-tank rifle apiece and the loopholes faced sideways with no frontal view...'

He visited the Maginot Line at Mont de Welshe and found the fortifications impressive, proof against frontal assault, but what of its being incomplete? On his return to London Reitz was grudgingly granted an

ABOVE **General Sir Edmund Ironside, Chief of the Imperial General Staff (left) and General the Viscount Gort, Commander-in-Chief of the British Expeditionary Force, with General Maurice Gamelin, who had just bestowed the Legion of Honour on his British allies, and General Joseph Georges.**
(IWM F2083)

MAIN PICTURE **Villy la Ferté, the most westerly of the Maginot Line fortresses, looking north-east. The dark patches in the middle distance to the left are girders planted to form anti-tank barriers. More turrets can be seen to the left of the dismounted one in the foreground, marking the far side of the fort.** (MME WW2/6/30)

interview by Neville Chamberlain and expressed his view that the Germans would go through the Escault line, the extension section east of Lille along the river of that name, like a knife through cheese. Chamberlain turned his observations aside with vague remarks. Clearly he and his colleagues did not want to be confused by the facts.

BELOW **The Schiesseck bunker, 100 kilometers (60 miles) east of Metz, photographed in August 1940.** (B82/46/30A)

THE NORTHERN FLANK – PLAN D

It was the task of General Maurice Gamelin, Commander-in-Chief of the French land forces, to decide what was to be done about the northern front. This was the way the Germans had come last time when the Schlieffen plan in modified form brought them sweeping round anti-clockwise through Belgium to threaten Paris. Given the solid bastion of the Maginot Line, this was what, presumably, they would have to do again. The trouble was that Belgium, fearful of a new invasion, had declared her neutrality and no joint policy could be formed with her. Thus the choice lay between defending the Belgian border with France, or entering Belgium when the Germans invaded (and thus when the French would be welcome) to halt the incursion on Belgian soil. Matters were further complicated by the uncertain position of the Dutch. The Netherlands had contrived to remain neutral in the First World War and clearly hoped to repeat the performance should another war

take place. Should that not prove to be possible, she would rely on her waterways to create a moated stronghold against the enemy which her small army would be able to garrison.

At 68 years old, Gamelin was already of retirement age, and his experience was firmly based on the previous war. He had been on Joffre's staff in 1914 and became a divisional commander later in the war. Like his fellows in the higher ranks of the French army, he had been impressed by the rewards of a defensive

ABOVE **German AFVs at Granadella, Catalonia. Valuable experience was gained by the Germans in the use of armour as a result of their participation in the Spanish Civil War.** (TM 4988/A/2)

ABOVE **German AFVs at Granadella, Catalonia. Valuable experience was gained by the Germans in the use of armour as a result of their participation in the Spanish Civil War.** (TM 4988/A/2)

BELOW RIGHT **A vision that haunted all who had served on the Western Front in the First World War. This tank, G46 commanded by Captain D. G. Browne in the Ypres salient on 31 July 1917, was stopped by the mud alone; the damage seen was the result of subsequent shelling. Guderian's strictures (see page 14) on choice of terrain were based on experience.** (TM 867/A4)

OPPOSITE RIGHT **German Panzer IAs on manoeuvres in 1939.** (TM 2894/B/4)

them. General Gaston Billotte, commanding First Army Group and responsible for the allied left as far as Sedan, was asked to look into this and was supported by his superior officer, the C-in-C North-east Front, General Joseph Georges, in resisting the plan.

The final decision grew out of a curious incident. On 9 January 1940 a German aircraft, an Me-108, came down near Mechelin, a little way north of Maastricht, having strayed in bad weather. One of the occupants, Major Hellmuth Reinberger, had a briefcase stuffed with secret papers relating to the planned invasion of Belgium and the Netherlands. He was unable to destroy all of them on capture and the Belgian authorities passed the information to the French and the Dutch. Although the Belgians did not go as far as to admit their friends to their territory, the information led to the adoption of the modified Dyle-Breda Plan on 20 March. This provided for 30 divisions, the cream of First Army Group, to thrust forward to the Dyle and beyond, with the French Seventh Army under General Henri Giraud rushing along the Belgian coast to link with the Dutch. Two of the three French armoured divisions would be involved and all three Light Mechanised Divisions (DLMs), which were actually not light at all. A DLM was armed to the level of a Panzer Division, having, typically, 80 Somua S35s, 80 Hotchkiss H35s, 60 Renault AMR33 light tanks and 40 Panhard P-178 armoured cars. The BEF, as a minor part of this manoeuvre, was to take up positions due east of the Belgian capital, Brussels.

approach in the past and now saw his task as the selection of a defensive position against which a German attack would fail. The first scheme, promulgated on 25 October, was to man a line from Antwerp southwards, along the Scheldt (in France becoming the Escaut) River, through Ghent and Tournai, but this left Brussels out and Plan D, to take up position on the little River Dyle, further east, on a line through Louvain and south to Namur and Dinant, was ordered on 15 November. That, however, left the Dutch out of the partnership and Gamelin toyed with the idea of pushing north of Antwerp to link with

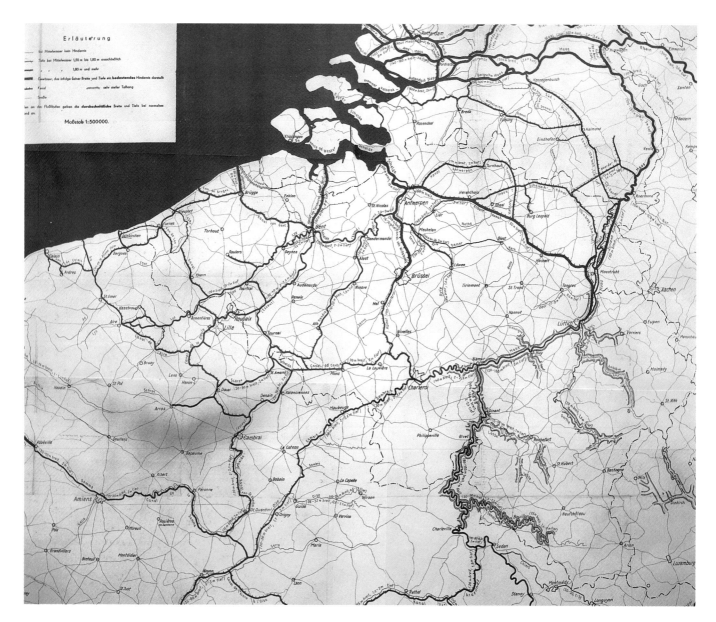

FALL GELB

While all this planning was going on, nothing much else was. The Germans, with their Soviet allies, had finished the conquest of Poland with chilling efficiency in precisely four weeks. In doing so they had added valuable new lessons to those already learned in the Spanish Civil War. In particular, the need to overcome the reluctance of front line commanders to keep moving ahead and the absolute necessity of increasing the proportion of more heavily armoured tanks, Panzer IIIs, against the thin-skinned Panzer Is. The German leader, Adolf Hitler, was all eagerness to attack the Allies in November, but, to the vast relief of his generals, was dissuaded by a combination of truth – the need to re-equip and bring more formations to combat readiness – and incompetence – the plans offered up for the attack.

The original German plan, *Fall Gelb*, (Case Yellow) was based on breaching Belgian neutrality with a thrust towards Ghent. What was to happen after that was not contemplated. It was a plan of so little inspiration and so easily countered that it is surprising that it was given credence by the Allies, let alone the Germans. Even this plan was reluctantly assembled by the German High Command, OKH (*Oberkommando des Heeres*), which was convinced that sufficient strength to overcome France could not be assembled before 1942. The plan was rejected and sent back for reworking. The ferocious winter then put matters on hold. The time gained not only allowed the army to build itself for the coming struggle, it also allowed an alternative plan to evolve.

THE THINKERS

The grand plans of both sides were being made by the established leaders, the men who had experienced

OPPOSITE LEFT **A map published, but with restricted circulation, by the German Generalstab des Heeres in 1939. It gives a schematic picture of waterways and their seriousness as obstacles, measurements of width and depth, in the southern Netherlands, Belgium and northern France. Hatching is used where rivers flow through deep gorges or below cliffs. Most place names are the same or similar in German, with the exception of Lüttich which most readers know as Liège.** (BL C28e1, MME WW2MapsMF2/14)

TOP **Panzer IBs were sent to Spain and still constituted a substantial proportion of German AFVs in 1940.** (Terry Hadler and Peter Sarson, *German Light Panzers 1932-1942*, New Vanguard 26)

BOTTOM **The first version of the Panzer IV, used in Poland in 1939. The white cross proved to offer too good an aiming mark and was soon painted over.** (Bruce Culver, *Panzerkampfwagen IV Medium Tank 1936-1945*, New Vanguard 28)

command in the previous European war. On the Allies' part, the French, who as the largest contributors of manpower had the upper hand in strategic planning, were set on defence, preferably in someone else's country, and the Germans had learned to fear the tenacity of the French soldier. Neither group had given sufficient attention to new ideas.

In September 1916 a practical indication of the way war was evolving had been given. The British used tanks to attack German positions at Flers in the Battle of the Somme. This was followed by the British attack at Arras in April 1917 and the French assault at Berry-au-Bac later the same month and, the outstanding demonstration of the weapon's potential, Cambrai in November. After the war such thinkers as J. F. C. Fuller, Basil Liddell Hart, E. D. Swinton and G. Le Q. Martel in Britain had kept both the technical development and the tactical use of armoured fighting vehicles alive as a subject of military interest. In France an officer attached to the Secrétariat Général de la Défence Nationale, an advisory body to the Prime Minister, offered his views in 1934 on a professional, mechanised force in a book entitled *Vers l'armée de métier*, translated into English in 1940 under the title *The Army of the Future*. Its author, Charles de Gaulle,

was given much the same respectful attention as his contemporaries over the English Channel; that is, virtually none.

In Germany equal thought was being given to the subject, and in 1937 Major-general Heinz Guderian, commander of the 2nd Panzer Division, published his book *Achtung! Panzer!* It did not appear in English until 1992. Guderian served much of the First World War in signals and became a radio specialist before becoming a staff officer. He then joined the staff of General E. Tschischwitz, head of Motor Transport Troops, and studied the use of motorised troop

formations, being driven to conclude that, alone, they were useless, but with artillery, engineers and tanks, the combination would be immensely powerful. Whether it was his background or his military genius that led Guderian to this vision of integrated operations involving tanks, artillery, engineers and mobile infantry is a moot point; what is important is that Guderian's views were to mould the strategy and tactics of the Panzer divisions. He specified three tactical requirements: surprise, deployment *en masse* and suitable terrain.

Of surprise he said:

'The rapid execution of the armoured attack is of decisive importance for the outcome of the battle; the supporting arms that are destined for permanent co-operation with the tanks must accordingly be just as fast-moving as the tanks themselves, and they must also be united with the tanks in an all-arms formation in peacetime.'

The principle of deployment en masse is, he stated, valid for all arms and as to terrain,

'the tank forces should be committed only where there are no obstacles that exceed the capacity of their machines; otherwise the armoured attack will break on the terrain.'

This was a truism that the strategists of the previous war had little difficulty in flouting, subsequently to assert that the tanks were useless. The only element missing from the array of forces Guderian discusses is the dive-bomber which is capable of fulfilling the function of artillery. The aircraft was seen, at the time of publication, as a reconnaissance tool and as a weapon to interdict reinforcement of the tanks' objectives.

Allied Order of Battle – 10 May 1940 (With names of commanders principally concerned. Units reading from north [left] to south [right])

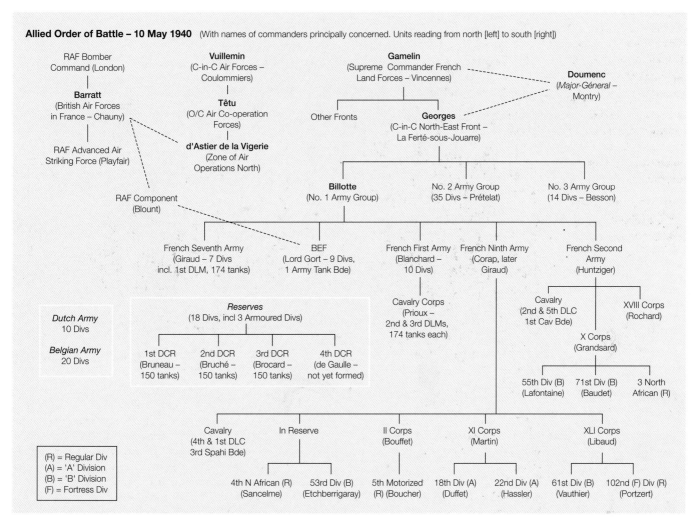

RAF Bomber
Command (London)
|
Barratt
(British Air Forces
in France – Chauny)
|
RAF Advanced Air
Striking Force (Playfair)

Vuillemin
(C-in-C Air Forces –
Coulommiers)
|
Têtu
(O/C Air Co-operation
Forces)
|
d'Astier de la Vigerie
(Zone of Air
Operations North)

Gamelin
(Supreme Commander French
Land Forces – Vincennes)

Doumenc
(*Major-Géneral* –
Montry)

Other Fronts

Georges
(C-in-C North-East Front –
La Ferté-sous-Jouarre)

RAF Component
(Blount)

Billotte
(No. 1 Army Group)

No. 2 Army Group
(35 Divs – Prételat)

No. 3 Army Group
(14 Divs – Besson)

French Seventh Army
(Giraud – 7 Divs
incl. 1st DLM, 174 tanks)

BEF
(Lord Gort – 9 Divs,
1 Army Tank Bde)

French First Army
(Blanchard –
10 Divs)

French Ninth Army
(Corap, later
Giraud)

French Second
Army
(Huntziger)

Dutch Army
10 Divs

Belgian Army
20 Divs

Reserves
(18 Divs, incl 3 Armoured Divs)

Cavalry Corps
(Prioux –
2nd & 3rd DLMs,
174 tanks each)

Cavalry
(2nd & 5th DLC
1st Cav Bde)

XVIII Corps
(Rochard)

X Corps
(Grandsard)

1st DCR
(Bruneau –
150 tanks)

2nd DCR
(Bruché –
150 tanks)

3rd DCR
(Brocard –
150 tanks)

4th DCR
(de Gaulle –
not yet formed)

55th Div (B)
(Lafontaine)

71st Div (B)
(Baudet)

3 North
African (R)

(R) = Regular Div
(A) = 'A' Division
(B) = 'B' Division
(F) = Fortress Div

Cavalry
(4th & 1st DLC
3rd Spahi Bde)

In Reserve

II Corps
(Bouffet)

XI Corps
(Martin)

XLI Corps
(Libaud)

4th N African (R)
(Sancelme)

53rd Div (B)
(Etchberrigaray)

5th Motorized
(R) (Boucher)

18th Div (A)
(Duffet)

22nd Div (A)
(Hassler)

61st Div (B)
(Vauthier)

102nd (F) Div (R)
(Portzert)

THE MANSTEIN PLAN

In October 1939 Colonel-general Gerd von Rundstedt, in command of Army Group A, had as his Chief-of-Staff Erich von Manstein, to whom he deferred in strategic planning. Neither of them were taken with the *Fall Gelb* proposals and they sought an alternative.

The Manstein plan – to cut the best mobile French and British troops off from their support and reserves by thrusting through to their south, and then to destroy them – was submitted to OKH in a memorandum countersigned by Rundstedt and dated 31 October 1939. It did not mention Sedan or the Ardennes, but did offer the destruction of the enemy. It was not welcome. OKH wanted time to increase the strength of the army and was mainly concerned with restraining Hitler. The meetings and arguments continued. In November Manstein summoned Guderian, now in command of XIX Panzer Corps, to discuss the possibility of passing a suitable force through the Ardennes to cross the river Meuse at Sedan and strike for Amiens. After careful consideration and study, Guderian assured Manstein that it was possible, provided the Panzers were present in sufficient strength; preferably the entire complement of Panzers in the German army.

The next memorandum, of early December, suggested that the principal use of the Germans' Panzer force should be on the Meuse. Shortly after this the errant aircraft with Major Reinberger blundered into Belgium, renewed foul weather delayed Gelb again and Hitler, appraised of the hornet's nest stirred up in Belgium and the Netherlands, cancelled Gelb for good. A new plan was demanded. The Allies' concept

of likely German plans was clear from their troop movements after the Mechelen incident, and Manstein, with characteristic arrogance, renewed his arguments for his plan. He was promptly posted to a new command as general of an infantry corps. Before he went a war game undertaken on 7 February tested the plan. It stood up well. A day or so later Colonel I. G. Schmundt, Hitler's chief adjutant, happened to visit Rundstedt's headquarters and Manstein had a chance to outline the plan to him. It was the first Hitler's staff had heard of it and the concept matched the Führer's own, but with added precision given by a trained military mind. A meeting between Hitler and Manstein was contrived, ostensibly to mark the occasion of his taking up his new command, and the morning of 17 February was spent in detailed discussion. Hitler then summoned the Commander-in-Chief of the army, Colonel-general Walter von Brauchitsch and Chief-of-Staff General Franz Halder to hear the astounding plan the Führer had devised. It could not, of course, be undertaken before late spring and an early summer campaign would follow. This suited OKH much better, and the army's recovery from the Polish campaign would also be nearly complete. A combination of chance and insight had given Germany a strategy that was to prove decisive.

SICHELSCHNITT

In Halder's hands Manstein's plan was taken to its logical conclusion. The operations of Army Group B under Colonel-general Fedor von Bock were to be a lure to draw the French and British north into Belgium. The action would have to be vigorous to be effective, but only three Panzer divisions, of which two

BELOW **An infantry tank Mark I of 4th RTR** (Peter Sarson, *Matilda Infantry Tank 1938-1945*, New Vanguard 8)

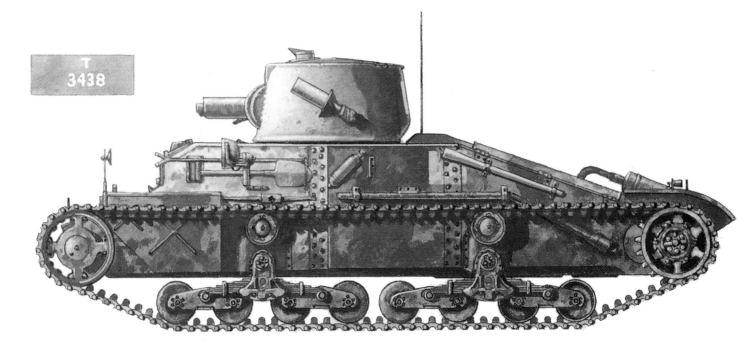

T 3438

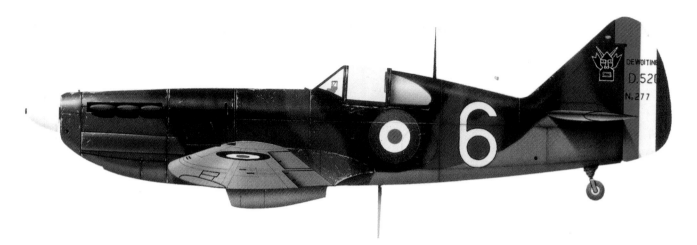

would be transferred to Rundstedt as soon as possible, were left to him and his force was, overall, reduced by a third to 29 divisions. In the east, opposite the Maginot Line, Wilhelm Ritter von Leeb's Army Group C with 19 divisions was to make much of itself to keep the French there in force. Meanwhile the 45 divisions of Army Group A, which included seven Panzer divisions, would deliver the major blow. The 'sickle-cut', sichelschnitt, would slice the Allies in two.

THE TANKS

The Treaty of Versailles ending the First World War had forbidden Germany to have tanks, so they were obviously much to be desired. The Germans therefore worked with the Russians and the Swedes in laying the foundations of what was to become a legendary force. By 1939 they had Panzer divisions equipped mainly with Panzerkampfwagen (PzKpfw) Is and IIs, the training and the reconnaissance AFVs. The former had a crew of two and was armed with twin 7.29mm machine-guns, was thinly armoured at 15mm, but was light and quick. The latter was even faster, had an additional crew member, heavier armour and substituted a 20mm cannon for one of the machine-guns. Neither could be considered formidable. To these had been added, after Hitler renounced the interdiction on tanks in 1935, the PzKpfw III, a serious improvement with a 50mm gun, two machine-guns, 30mm of armour and a crew of five and the PzKpfw IV which carried a 75mm gun and 43mm of armour. These were, however, much longer in the building than anticipated and were thus in short supply at the outbreak of war. The shortfall was filled to some extent by Czech designs taken over after the Germans had seized the country that developed them. The PzKpkw 35(t) and 38(t) had 37mm guns and four man crews. They were slightly more lightly armoured than the PzKpfw II and slower, but the additional crew gave them an advantage in fighting ability.

In May 1940 German tank strength stood at 523 PzKpfw Is, 955 PzKpfw IIs, 349 PzKpfw IIIs, 278 PzKpfw IVs, 106 35(t)s and 288 38(t)s. Some two-thirds of the force of 2,499 tanks were the light, vulnerable and trivially-armed Is and IIs.

The French AFVs were present in greater numbers with 3,285 tanks available. A third of these were scattered about as infantry support while the rest were divided between the DLMs and the new armoured divisions, the Divisions Cuirassées (DCRs). Two DCRs had been formed in January 1940 and the third in March. The 4th French Armoured was not in existence until the German invasion was already under way. The DLMs had Somua S35s, medium tanks with 40mm of armour and armed with a 47mm gun and a machine gun. Their Hotchkiss H35s had only 18mm of armour and a 37mm gun. The DCRs also had Hotchkiss tanks, but their chief weapon was the massive Renault B1bis, the *Char B*, with 80mm of armour, a 47mm gun in the turret on top and, mounted in the hull, an impressive 75mm gun. The great drawback of French tank design was that the turrets were small and the commander of the AFV had not only to control the tank, but also to serve and fire the gun. The hull-mounted weapon of the Char B could be elevated and depressed, but not traversed; the whole tank had to be turned. What is more, it was served by the driver. A final, fatal flaw was the positioning of the radiator grille on the flank of the tank. It might as well have been labelled 'I am vulnerable here, please shoot.' The Char B was, none the less, formidable.

The British contribution included 4th and 7th Battalions, Royal Tank Regiment, each with 50 Infantry Tanks Mark I, known as Matildas. These two-man tanks were heavily armoured, 60mm, and equipped with a machine gun. They were horribly slow, really no more than a shell-proof crawling machine-gun emplacement, and were introduced in February 1939. The prototype Mark I had stimulated the demand for a gun-carrying, faster version with a three-man crew. Only 23 of the 2-pounder (40mm) gunned Mark IIs had reached the army in May 1940. These battalions also had a small number of the

three-man light Mark VIs, with only 14mm of armour and two machine-guns, the AFV used by the seven British cavalry battalions with the BEF which had 28 of them each. The 1st Armoured Division started to arrive in France at Le Havre in May 1940, with one brigade in Mark VIs and a second with Cruiser tanks, lightly armoured but carrying a 2-pounder gun. Both these British tanks had top speeds equal to the best of the German AFVs at 30mph (50kmph).

Although attempts had been made to use wireless communication with tanks and aircraft in the First World War, the first practical wireless sets did not appear until 1926 when the British introduced radio-telephony (R/T) which carried voice messages over short ranges, morse code signals carried by wireless-telegraphy (W/T) being well-established and operating over quite long distances. The No.2 radio set of 1932 had a range, from a stationary tank, of 12 miles (19km). By the outbreak of the war the British were on the point of introducing the HF (high frequency) No.19 set, vastly improved, which had the added advantage of giving not only external communication with other tanks, but also internal communication with the crew. Guderian, already

experienced in radio, was well aware of the developments of the early 1930s, and in *Achtung! Panzer!* wrote:

'Radio … is the principal medium of control between tank units and the other forces, and radios are the main equipment of the signals elements which provide communication for the tank units and their supporting arms… Basically the signals elements maintain the communications between commanders and their sub-units, between commanders and their own superiors, and with whatever neighbouring forces, aircraft and other units are engaged in the common task. The signallers must remain in the closest contact with the commanders to whom they are assigned. In combat these commanders will be right up in front with their tanks, which means that armoured radio vehicles with full cross-country capability are essential for the panzer signals elements.'

The Germans used VHF (very high frequency) radios in tanks, as did the RAF in its aircraft. The French placed less emphasis on communication. At the outbreak of war only 20% of their tanks were fitted with radio sets.

However, it was still a fact that the Allied tank strength outnumbered the German by almost 1,000 units in May 1940. It was to be a case of the size of the weapon being less important than how it was used.

THE AIRCRAFT

In the air the Germans had numerical superiority, but not by a very large margin. The predictions of early 1939 proved to be inaccurate and where the Allies expected to have about 850 bombers available, France could produce about 175 and Britain some 220. The German strength was about three-quarters of the forecast 2,000 machines. In fighters the numbers were much as predicted; 1,000 German against 700 French and, in France, 130 British. As in the case of the bombers, Britain could fly additional sorties from home soil. In reconnaissance aircraft the Allies had something less than half the forecast at 400 or so against a German total of 500 but it was in the dive-bomber category, not even considered in the planning, that the Germans were generously equipped. They could put 342 such craft in the air, while the French had a mere 54 and the British had none at all.

The age and quality of the types being flown was of yet greater significance. The French fighters were relatively modern, the Morane 406, Bloch 152, the American Curtiss H-75 and, the jewel in the crown, the Dewoîtine D520, of which only 36 had been delivered on 10 May 1940. The French bombers were not modern at all. Nor, in truth, were the British bombers. The Fairey Battle had a crew of three and a top speed of 257mph (410kph) while the Bristol Blenheim IV was a little faster with 266mph. The German fighters, the single-engined Messerschmitt Bf109 and Bf110 had speeds of 357mph (575kph) and 336mph respectively. The British Hawker Hurricane, the backbone of the RAF, was capable of only 322mph (518kph), much the same as the Dewoîtine, while the Spitfire, which was flown only from England, was the fastest at 362mph (582kph), although other factors influence the superiority of one machine over another. Over France, however, the Germans clearly had the edge.

German Dornier 17Zs were used for high altitude photo-reconnaissance as well as bombing and the Heinkel He 111H formed half of the force that went into action on 10 May. The dive-bombers included the older Henschel Hs 123A but the Junkers Ju87B, the Stuka had the greatest impact on Allied troops. It was actually fairly slow with a top speed of 242mph (390kph) so that it depended on being unopposed in the air, as so often it was, or well protected by Messerschmitts. Thus while numerical superiority existed, it was more in the field of technical excellence that the German advantage lay in air warfare.

THE PHONEY WAR

As both sides built their strength, one for defence and one for attack, troop inactivity appeared to be the outstanding characteristic of the war – hence the wry American adjective. The French had made a feeble foray into the Saarland in September 1939, but had hustled home as the Polish resistance failed. No attempt was made to take the battle to the Germans, much to the relief of the OKH. The BEF under the command of Lord Gort was kept entertained with the

LEFT **Bored French troops in Chaumont, south of Sedan, amused themselves by carving names in the stonework of the houses. This 'Caverne des Grognards' makes use of the nickname 'grognards' or grumblers adopted by Napoleon's Old Guard.** (MME WW2/6/18)

construction of defences and vigorous training which was to stand it in good stead later.

For all the apparent inaction, people were still in danger of getting killed. C. N. Barker, a Second Lieutenant in the 1st Gordon Highlanders went from digging trenches on the Belgian frontier to join the 51st (Highland) Division when his battalion, regular soldiers, was sent to stiffen the territorials of the 51st on the Saar front. He wrote explaining that the interval defences of the Maginot Line were organised into the *Ligne de Contact*, the forward position, and the *Ligne de Receuil*, to which one fell back.

'The Ligne de Contact consisted of a number of dispersed platoon positions in the woods on the frontier. Having previously reconnoitred the position in daylight we moved forward in the dark with a French guide. My platoon position was in the very isolated position in a wood separated from the rest of the company called Le Petit Wolscher. We moved silently forward trying to make no sound and eventually arrived at what appeared Western style stockades known as froggeries! Most of the structure was above ground, it was constructed of logs,

heavily wired, situated close to the very edge of the wood facing the Germans. The relief was quickly carried out and the French departed leaving us in a very lonely spot. By day it was quiet we patrolled our wood regularly to ensure there was no infiltration. At night it was quite different our sentries listened intently for enemy patrols, owls hooted, an animal moved in the undergrowth and a tin filled with pebbles to give warning of movement alerted us, our antenna was at full stretch. During one night after a long vigil I distinctly remember the Queen Mary sailing by. Strange things happen to one in such circumstances. Another night a patrol approached our position and up went an SOS flare but down came a curtain of protective artillery fire from the French soixante-quinze battery. We were not unduly upset, but we were relieved at this outpost and withdrawn to the Ligne de Receuil. A few days later the German offensive began, the outpost was overrun and its occupants either killed or taken prisoner, such are the fortunes of war.'

Where there was no danger during the winter of 1939-1940, there was the cold. It was one of the worst winters in living memory and ice and snow prevented

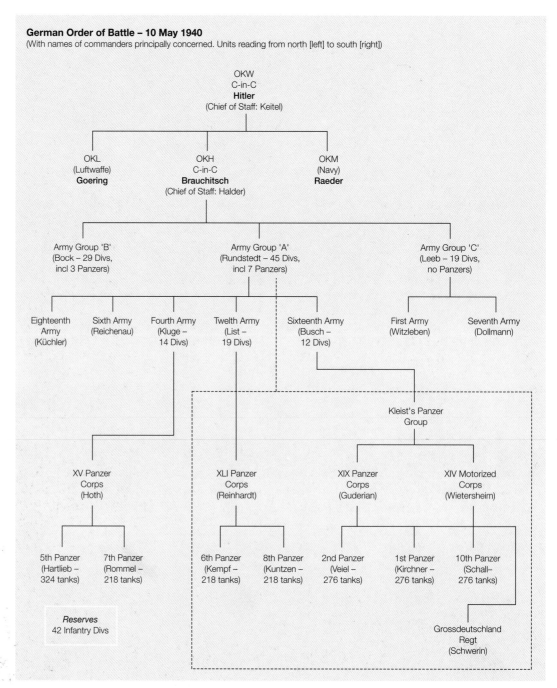

German Order of Battle – 10 May 1940
(With names of commanders principally concerned. Units reading from north [left] to south [right])

OKW
C-in-C
Hitler
(Chief of Staff: Keitel)

OKL
(Luftwaffe)
Goering

OKH
C-in-C
Brauchitsch
(Chief of Staff: Halder)

OKM
(Navy)
Raeder

Army Group 'B'
(Bock – 29 Divs,
incl 3 Panzers)

Army Group 'A'
(Rundstedt – 45 Divs,
incl 7 Panzers)

Army Group 'C'
(Leeb – 19 Divs,
no Panzers)

Eighteenth Army
(Küchler)

Sixth Army
(Reichenau)

Fourth Army
(Kluge –
14 Divs)

Twelfth Army
(List –
19 Divs)

Sixteenth Army
(Busch –
12 Divs)

First Army
(Witzleben)

Seventh Army
(Dollmann)

Kleist's Panzer Group

XV Panzer
Corps
(Hoth)

XLI Panzer
Corps
(Reinhardt)

XIX Panzer
Corps
(Guderian)

XIV Motorized
Corps
(Wietersheim)

5th Panzer
(Hartlieb –
324 tanks)

7th Panzer
(Rommel –
218 tanks)

6th Panzer
(Kempf –
218 tanks)

8th Panzer
(Kuntzen –
218 tanks)

2nd Panzer
(Veiel –
276 tanks)

1st Panzer
(Kirchner –
276 tanks)

10th Panzer
(Schall–
276 tanks)

Reserves
42 Infantry Divs

Grossdeutschland
Regt
(Schwerin)

a good deal of the planned work on defences. Gunner Albert Smith was with 159 (Lloyds) Battery, 53rd City of London Regiment, RA (Ack-ack). His unit was protecting an airfield of the British Advanced Air Striking Force near Reims. Their clothing, second-hand to start with, was First World War issue – riding breeches lacing up at the calf, puttees and summer weight coats. They huddled in half-sunken steel shelters, cooking in the open.

Many of the French regiments, composed of conscripts and reservists, became ill-disciplined. Boredom and drunkenness were seriously damaging to morale in such units. Lieutenant-general Alan Brooke,

commander of 2nd Corps, BEF, attended a parade on 11 November 1939 with General Corap, French Ninth Army. He recalled:

'I can see those troops now. Seldom have I seen anything more slovenly and badly turned out. Men unshaven, horses ungroomed, clothes and saddlery that did not fit ... What shook me most, however, was the look in the men's faces, disgruntled and insubordinate ...'

Although it was important to avoid a breach of Belgian neutrality, the requirements of Plan D, the advance to the River Dyle if and when the Germans invaded, made knowledge of the ground a necessity. Secret missions to acquire the intelligence were undertaken. In March 1940, for example, the late Major-general F. H. N. Davidson had been sent in civilian clothes and with a civilian passport to Brussels, ostensibly to deliver a diplomatic bag. He then spent some days being driven about, peering out of a car window, determining the actual state of the alleged anti-tank defences (woeful) and checking the accuracy of their maps (deficient). Much was gained by such visits but it was deeply unsatisfactory to be constrained to behave thus when one's troops were likely to be asked to put their lives at risk.

While the war may have been phoney, it was not safe. British regiments were sent on tours of duty as interval troops on the Maginot Line. The 51st (Highland) Division set off for the Saar front in late April. The action was a series of petty but lethal encounters as Army Goup C fulfilled its mission of keeping the attention of the French fixed on this front. The 51st were not inclined to tolerate too much peace and adopted an aggressive patrol style. On 7 May 4th Black Watch were attacked and surrounded in the village of Betting but were relieved. The next day their whole brigade was the object of German attention, artillery followed by sustained infantry attacks. Private J. McCready of 1st Black Watch wrote with some relish:

'Price and Fisher had an excellent time with a Bren gun and a rifle, their bag of the enemy was put down as 44 in an afternoon. It was all storm-troopers in that action, but the Black Watch was more than a match for them, they proved nothing better than good target practice as some of the boys said.'

The 4th Cameron Highlanders had become aware of German line-tapping jeopardising the security of their telephone communications. They responded by speaking in Gaelic.

Far to the west Despatch Rider Stanley Rayner of 2/6th East Surrey Regiment, a native of Selby in Yorkshire, had arrived in Le Havre early in May 1940. His battalion was billeted at Rouelles, just north of the town, at a château. In fact most of the men were in bell tents in the grounds. Rayner and friends decided to investigate the local scene.

'... the 'lads' were talking of going down to see Le Havre – what for? well they had heard about the Red Light District there... Quite a number of us ambled along though Rouelles to find some sort of bus to explore this novelty, out of curiosity of course... Rue de Galleon ... Having viewed all the establishments from the outside where some old crone who looked old enough to have been in the French Revolution ... was calling out in English

BELOW **28 October 1939: British Bren gun carriers moving up to the front.** (TM 1417/C/5)

… *"pretty girls inside, Tommy, pretty girls inside." We went in to buy a drink… Anything drinkable, or perhaps not, was there for the buying at the price, as I found to my cost, of about three times dearer than the cafés in Rouelles. As we sat there drinking a beer, one of these smashing looking young things came and sat on my knee. Heck I wasn't used to this so I pushed her onto the man alongside where she sat and had a chinwag. Apparently they would go on the 'Game' for about five years then retire with enough to buy a milliners shop in a provincial town … and marry someone or other.'*

A FINAL HANDICAP

The British came under General Georges's North-East Front command which had its headquarters at La Ferté-sous-Jouarre, 40 miles (65km) east of Paris. From 6 January 1940 Georges himself reported to General Gamelin, whose HQ was at Vincennes on the eastern edge of the capital, but at the same time a new entity was created, GHQ Land Forces under General Aimé Doumenc halfway between the two at Montry, and interposed in the command structure as well. Various key functions of the Staff were likewise scattered about between the three headquarters.

RIGHT **Men of the 1st Loyal Regiment demonstrate the new radio-telephone equipment.** (IWM F3081)

ABOVE **Preparations for an
earlier war, the neatly-dug
trenches well-suited to
1914-18, are inspected by
the British Leader of the
Opposition, Clement Attlee, in
the winter snow.** (IWM F2055)

Number 1 Army Group, responsible for the front from the North Sea to the start of the Maginot Line east of Sedan, was commanded by General Gaston Billotte. The Group consisted, from west to east, of the French 7th Army under General Henri Giraud, the BEF, the French 1st Army under General Georges Blanchard, the French 9th Army under General André Corap and the French 2nd Army under General Charles Huntziger. The BEF included an RAF Air Component consisting of two squadrons of Hurricanes, two of Gloster Gladiator biplane fighters, four of Blenheims, five of Lysander artillery spotting aircraft and one of Dragon Rapides for liaison. This was under the command of Air Vice-Marshal C. H. B. Blount who reported to Air Marshal A. S. Barratt, commanding British Air Forces in France, to whom Air Vice-Marshal P. H. L. Playfair, the commander of another unit, RAF Advanced Air Striking Force, also reported. The latter formation consisted of eight Battle squadrons, two of Blenheims and two of Hurricanes. While operational control remained with Gort, command stretched back to the RAF in Britain.

André Maurois reported a conversation he had with General Giraud who observed to him:

'It's a most regrettable fact, but we're short of everything … aircraft! Do you know how many aeroplanes I, the Commander of an Army, have at my disposal? Eight. Just eight. I know of course that there's the Royal Air Force and that it's excellent, but if I want to make a reconnaissance I have to ask General Georges who asks General Gamelin, who asks Marshal Barratt, who asks Vice-Marshal Blount, who has a reconnaissance made for me, but more often than not long after it would have been of any real use.'

The French Air Force was not under Gamelin's control at all, but was commanded by an officer responsible to the Minister of Defence. The Commander-in-Chief of l'Armée de l'Air was General Joseph Vuillemin to whom, fortunately, Barratt had been liaison officer before his new appointment. Barratt wisely established his headquarters next to Vuillemin's and made an admirable job of reconciling the vague and confusing directives and command structures imposed upon him.

The confusion was compounded by the primitive means of communication. The high command rushed about in large motor cars to meet and eat lunch, a procedure that would become less convenient when under attack. Written messages were carried by despatch rider and resort was made to the telephone. Vincennes, Gamelin's headquarters from which the overall control of the Allied land forces emanated, was innocent of any sort of radio transmitter/receiver. Should land lines be compromised by enemy advance, alternative lines had to be used. Eventually Paris would be forced to communicate with Dunkirk by means of a link through London.

Upon this shaky, ill-defined and poorly-equipped chain of command the Allied war effort depended. At its summit was the French Cabinet, a nest of unrest and intrigue, which communicated fitfully with the British Cabinet, an organ that operated in sad ignorance of the actual state of affairs beyond their shores.

NORWAY

Attention was deflected from France and the Low Countries on 9 April 1940 when Germany overran Denmark and landed in Norway. The Norwegians fought bravely, but the Allies had been taken by surprise. The Royal Navy sank the German destroyers protecting the Narvik landings between 10 and 13 April, but it was not until 15 April that the first British land troops arrived there. The first French troops arrived in Norway on 19 April. The Allied response further south was feeble and the Germans had soon ferried in enough troops by air to have secured central and southern Norway, though at the cost of 10 of their 20 destroyers and three of their eight cruisers, a body blow to the German navy. But worse damage had been done to the Allies. The British had been out-manoeuvred in a maritime campaign, to the scarcely-concealed amusement of the French, while the position of Gamelin in France became extremely insecure and he only escaped the sack because Prime Minister Paul Reynaud, stricken with influenza, was unable to out-manoeuvre Defence Minister Edouard Daladier. In Britain on 9 May Parliament debated the failure in Norway and Prime Minister Neville Chamberlain was forced to resign. On 10 May Winston Churchill replaced him. The first news to reach the new leader was of the German invasion of the Netherlands and Belgium.

BELOW **The Indian Expeditionary Force landing at Marseille.** (IWM F2005)

THE STORMING OF THE LOW COUNTRIES

The Netherlands is not as flat as usually supposed, but is a good deal smaller than. From the German border east of Nijmegen to Rotterdam is a mere 60 miles (100km). Along the Belgian border and curling north on the west of the Maas (Meuse) is a ridge of higher land broken only where the Waal and Lower Rhine, which is joined by the IJssel from the north, pass through the gap between Nijmegen and Arnhem to run westwards. These rivers join the sea in a complex of channels and islands with Rotterdam on the northern shore.

The defence of the country could only depend on the waterways, for in the country cupped by the hills the land drops to a level below that of the sea, protected by the dunes and dykes that run north from Rotterdam to the long dyke that encloses the IJsselmeer (Zuider Zee). At the heart of the country *Vesting Holland*, Fortress Holland, embraced Amsterdam, the Hague and Rotterdam. It was defended on a line from Muiden, east of Amsterdam, southwards, passing east of Utrecht and reaching the Waal at Gorinchem where the line turned south-west to include the island of Hoekschewaard (Hoekse Waard) north of the waterway crossed by the Moerdijk bridge. In the extreme north the IJsselmeer dyke was protected by massive blockhouses which were to hold out for the duration of hostilities. In the south-west the complex of islands, Zeeland, protecting the approaches to Vlissingen (Flushing) and Antwerp were treated as an independent defence zone.

The strategy was based on falling back to Fortress Holland from a forward line along the Maas and then from a line some 10 miles (16km) to the west along the little river Raam and through the Peel region to join the Maas south of Roermond. This line extended north as the Valley position west of Wageningen to the IJsselmeer at Naarden. These lines were chosen to follow rivers or canals, or to be supplemented by flooding the land, but the need to withdraw meant preserving bridges until the latest possible moment.

BELOW **German paratroops descend near the Moerdijk Bridge. The picture is said to date from 10 May 1940, but may be from a subsequent re-enactment made for a propaganda film.** (Boersma)

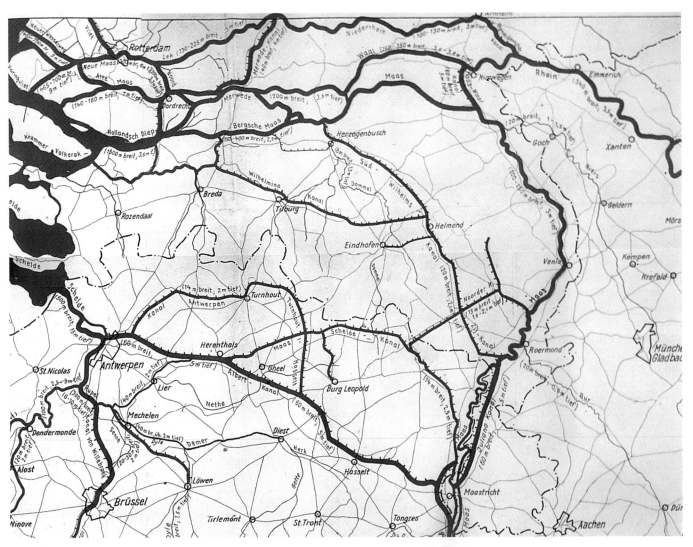

ABOVE **The Netherlands section of the Germans' waterways map of 1939 shown in full on page 12.**

DANZIG

On 3 May 1940 Colonel Hans Oster, a senior German officer, told his friend, the Dutch Military Attaché in Berlin, Colonel Sas, that an attack was imminent. Sas had been acquiring excellent intelligence from this source for some time. They met again on the evening of Thursday, 9 May, at 9.30 p.m. A single code-word, *Danzig*, had been transmitted to the German forces half an hour before; the attack was to proceed. Sas had some difficulty in persuading his chiefs in The Hague that the information was sound, and it was not until 3 a.m. on the morning of 10 May that they started to blow the bridges over the Maas.

The bridges were obviously crucial to the defence. The German efforts to seize them were not, therefore, limited to assault but also attempted guile. Units known by the cover name of Brandenburgers had been prepared for use in the Sudetenland, and also in Poland. By means of disguise they were to infiltrate and capture key locations. Dressed in Dutch uniforms, the Brandenburgers now advanced on the Maas bridges. In Maastricht they failed, but further north, at Gennep, it was a different story. Oberleutnant Wilhelm Walther's 4 Kompanie approached the bridge there, which carried the railway at that time, together with two Dutch members of the Nationaal Socialistische Beweging, a pro-Nazi party. They hid there until dawn when two German trains rolled towards the station, which had been taken by another party of Brandenbergers. Walther's men were marched onto the bridge by their fake captors, the Dutch in military uniform, and overpowered the guards, preventing the bridge from being blown as the German train came up. The railway line continued to Uden, and the Germans were thus able to penetrate the Raam-Peel Line as far as a railway halt called Zeeland with two train-loads of troops as early as 4 a.m. on Friday 10 May. Elsewhere on the line of the Maas Dutch resistance was more effective, but by the end of the day all those who had not been overcome by the Germans were in full retreat to the Zuid Willems canal between 's-Hertogenbosch and Helmond.

THE AIRBORNE ASSAULT

While the attack on their borders was expected and was dealt with, with greater or less success, as planned, the Dutch were surprised and shaken by the attack from the air. They had, naturally, placed the greater part of their forces on the principal defence lines, and Rotterdam, for example, was no more than a supply depot. It was into the lightly manned heartland of Fortress Holland that the German airborne strike was directed. Under General-leutnant Kurt Student, 3,500 paratroops of 7th Airborne Division were the vanguard to 12,000 men from 22nd Infantry Division airlifted into the area.

The southern front was attacked by a drop of 700 men both north and south of the Moerdijk bridges which were taken without significant resistance. The detonators to the demolition charges were not even in place despite the hour, 6.40 a.m. The principal waterway defence of the southern flank was already in German hands. The drops in Dordrecht, south of the town and on the bridges, were equally successful. The attack on Rotterdam was carried out with similar efficiency with 700 paratroops taking Waalhaven, although some men fell into the burning buildings

that had been ignited by their own bombs. The airlift was hampered by Dutch anti-aircraft fire as, at 7.00 a.m., they started to bring in the infantry and Student with his staff. Harassing fire from artillery north of the river continued through the day and Dutch and British air-raids went on into the following night.

The most remarkable landing at Rotterdam took place on the river. A dozen Heinkel He 59 sea-planes brought 120 men of the 16th Infantry into the centre of the city, four landing downstream of the bridges and making for the northern end of the bridges while some of those landing upstream actually put their men ashore at the quay in front of the railway station. A Dutch policeman, Ben Raes, who attempted to arrest some of the Germans, was killed. The rest of the upstream arrivals taxied into Koningshaven and took the bridges south of the island before joining their comrades coming from the north. These troops were reinforced by another 50 who landed at a sports stadium in Feyenoord and commandeered a tram to carry them up to the bridges. On the northern bank the Dutch reaction was immediate. A company of the 39th Infantry pushed the north-western development of the German bridgehead back towards the river

BELOW **Detail from the German Generalstab des Heeres Belgian military geography road map, published in Berlin in October 1939. The railway line runs across the lower part of the map, south of Gennep towards Uden. The Peel line came south from Grave along the Raam. The railway halt to which the Germans advance by train is shown by a square south of Zeeland.** (BL C28e1, MME WW2Maps/3/23)

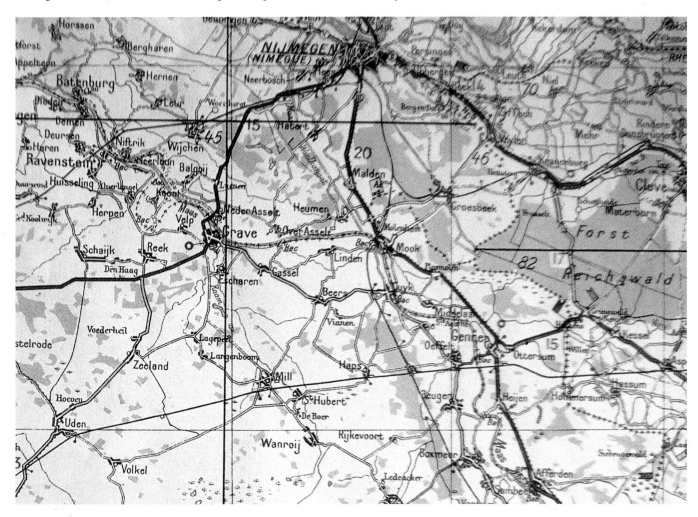

RIGHT **The Germans landed at Waalhaven airfield in south-west Rotterdam where preliminary bombing had set buildings on fire.** (B 80/15/32)

BELOW **To seize the bridges over the river some men were landed by seaplane. Twelve Heinkel He 59s brought 120 men to land on the banks of the Maas.** (Nederlands Instituut voor Oorlogsdocumentatie)

while some Dutch Marines opened fire from the Maashotel, and then stopped an attempted advance towards the Buers railway station. Meanwhile, from the river, the *Z-5*, a Dutch gun-boat and the *TM-51* torpedo boat shot up the seaplanes and exchanged fire with the Germans before, towards noon, they ran out of ammunition and withdrew. That afternoon the destroyer *Van Galen* attempted to sail up the river to join the battle but was hit and severely damaged by Stukas; she later sank.

To the north of Rotterdam the Germans were less successful. The airports of Schipol, Bergen, Waalhaven, de Kooy, Sosterberg, Haastede and Hilversum had all been bombed in the early hours and after a bomb attack at 3.30 a.m. the airfield at Valkenburg, south of Katwijk aan Zee, was attacked. The German aircraft flew over and on out to sea, towards England. Then they turned back to take the Dutch by surprise. One hundred and twenty men of Fallschirm-Jäger Regiment (FJR) 2 dropped there. The garrison, part of 3rd Battalion, 4th Infantry Brigade, was ejected but when the Ju 52s carrying the German reinforcements arrived, the runway proved to be too soft. The aircraft that landed bogged down and blocked the way for others. Some 26 Junkers attempted to put down on the beach between Katwijk and Scheveningen (on the northern outskirts of The Hague) of which only six took off again to return to base. Five Fokker C-Xs of the Dutch Army Air Force attacked the airfield with bombs and strafed the beach,

Herinnering Nederland 10 Mei 1940

ABOVE LEFT **Paratroops jump from a low-flying Junkers JU 52.** (Boersma)

LEFT **Over Ypenburg parachutes fill the sky.** (Boersma)

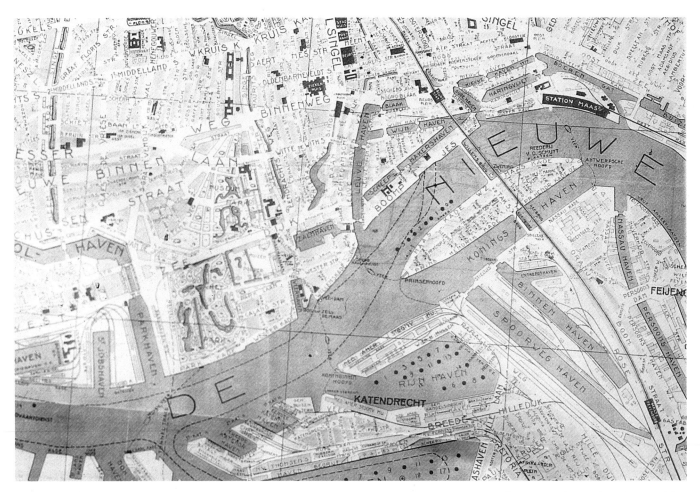

ABOVE **Detail from the 1939 German map of Rotterdam, showing how the waterways restrict movement around the bridges.** (BL C29:25 Rotterdam [1], WW2Maps3/19)

3rd Battalion, 4th Infantry returned to the attack and 3rd Brigade, 2nd Artillery shelled Valkenburg field. The Dutch brought raw recruits up from 2nd Infantry Depot at Leiden, but, not surprisingly, they contributed little against crack German units. The battle was further confused by civilian interventions. The Blue Tram came stridently on the scene on its way from Katwijk, ringing its bell furiously, its passengers eagerly viewing the fight and loath to miss a moment of this 'fresh, jolly war.' A little later a farm girl came stolidly along on her bicycle. Both sides ceased fire to allow her to pass. In the midst of the conflict local farmers testily asked the Dutch commander when he would be finished as they wanted to milk the cows. By 5.30 p.m. the airfield had been regained and the Germans had taken up defensive positions near Wassenaar and in Valkenburg village.

The drop at Ockenburg, south-west of The Hague, went yet worse for the Germans. The paratroops were widely dispersed, some so isolated that they were forced to hide for days until the Dutch eventually surrendered. Others managed to reach the airfield, but once more the runway was soon blocked by incoming aircraft. By 1.30 p.m. 1st Battalion, Brigade of Grenadiers had retaken the position, taking some 130 prisoners and forcing the remaining

Germans to defend themselves as best they could at Ockenrode.

The third drop was to the east of The Hague at Ypenburg. Anti-aircraft fire broke up the approaching formation and the paratroops were scattered far from the airfield, with the result that the transport aeroplanes were shot down on their attempting to land by armoured cars stationed there. Subsequent waves of transports ran into similar trouble. One of them was hit and crashed in the city where documents retrieved from it revealed plans to capture the Dutch Royal Family and other dignitaries. The paratroops regrouped and managed to capture part of Ypenburg airport, but they were attacked by 2nd and 3rd Battalions, Brigade of Grenadiers and were pushed out again. Ignorant of the fact, Hurricanes of 32 Squadron RAF attacked at 5 p.m. and reported that they had destroyed the Ju 52s there, actually the wrecks of aircraft shot up earlier by the Dutch.

At 7.30 p.m. the Germans signalled to their headquarters that the landings at Katwijk, Kijduin and Ypenburg had largely failed due to strong ground and air defences. Valkenburg was in German hands. The fate of a number of units was unknown. The German forces north of Rotterdam were in desperate state, while those south of the city and on the bridges were holding their own, but not without hardship. A German soldier reported:

'At 19.00 the 12th company covers us in a smoke screen… Yet another is lying there on a stretcher, our young lieutenant, shot in the stomach. "Commandant, it's going really badly, no-one can get through that," he said with his last strength, then fell back. But still, we attack again. We have to keep control of this bridgehead… On the opposite side the bank is brightly lit. It is dark already. By 22.00 it gets quieter. Over there everything is ablaze.'

Meanwhile, to the east, the German advance was proceeding. On the right, in the north of the country, progress was swift until the Germans found themselves up against the Kornwerderzand blockhouse at the eastern end of the great dyke on the IJsselmeer, beyond which they failed to make any advance. South of that wide body of water they were pushing west, and, further south again, the Dutch Light Division and the 3rd Army Corps had been ordered back to Fortress Holland. The Dutch Commander-in-Chief, General Henri G. Winkelman, needed them to dislodge the Germans at Waalhaven and on the bridges to the south. This meant the area to the rear of the Raam-Peel Line would be undefended, and that the Light Division had to make its way north from Tilburg across the Maas and the Waal before turning west. In

Belgium, Plan D was in force, and so the French 7th Army under General Giraud was hurrying towards the Netherlands and their motorised troops would cross the border with Belgium early the next day. The 6th Cuirassiers had to beg fuel from the Belgians and clear the obstacles the Belgians had erected on the Dutch border in order to maintain their pace.

THE SECOND AND FINAL DAYS

The relief of Rotterdam went badly. The French were bombed away from the Hollands Diep, across which the Moerdijk bridges pass, and the Dutch Light Division was halted on the River Noord at Alblasserdam, north of Dordrecht. Meanwhile the reinforcement of the German forces at Rotterdam continued for, although the Waalhaven airport was useless, German pilots managed to put down on the car park area of Feyenoord and on the Dordrecht to Moerdijk road. The Dutch fronts to the north round the IJsselmeer were holding, and the German troops around The Hague were reduced to defending the little enclaves to which the Dutch had reduced them.

In Valkenburg the citizens took what shelter they could find from their countrymen's bombardment of the German occupiers. Mr de Wilde, the mayor, telephoned Lieutenant-colonel Buurman, commander

BELOW **The southern approaches to Rotterdam from from the German Generalstab des Heeres Belgian military geography road map, published in Berlin in October 1939. The Moerdijk bridges are between Dordrecht and Breda.** (BL C28e1, MME WW2Maps/3/20)

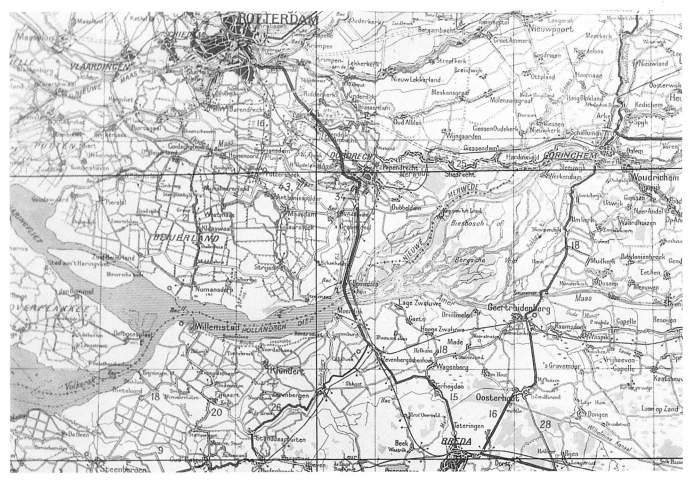

ABOVE **Aircraft landing at Valkenburg sank into the grass airstrip and blocked it for further landings. Some days later Mr G. Koenen and his friends went to see the JU 52s and he made this photograph. In due time the 14-year-old girl second from right, Adriana v.d. Zaal, became Mrs Koenen.** (Photo G. Koenen, Wassenaar)

RIGHT **Attempts to land on the beach near Wassenaar led to crashes and to attack by the Dutch Air Force.** (Photo A. C. Duijvestijn)

of the Dutch 4th Infantry surrounding the town, to ask him to cease firing, but nothing came of that. The next day, Sunday 12 May, in the afternoon, a shell hit a German ammunition lorry that was standing outside a café. Attempts by the Dutch to take the town were frustrated by Oberleutnant Voigt with 140 men in the dunes by the Wassenaarse Slag when the advancing troops presumed they were under fire from their comrades and failed to take appropriate action. On Monday the church, in which civilians were sheltering, was set on fire. The Dutch pressure would not cease until the order came to lay down their arms and the inhabitants of Valkenburg suffered accordingly.

German success now depended on a single, major factor: 9th Panzer Division. The Gennep crossing served the German armour well on 11 May. By the afternoon the tanks were at the Zuid Willems canal at Veghel which they crossed and by the next morning they were to the north of Tilburg. The forward reconnaissance forces of the French were encountered between there and Breda, but offered no serious check to progress. By late on Sunday 12 May the Moerdijk bridges had been reached and the land-line to the isolated paratroopers was secure. The balance of 9th Panzer crossed the Moerdijk bridges the next day and on 14 May General Student was shaking hands with the Panzer leader, Generalmajor Alfred von Hubicki. The bridges had not been too far, but it was a close-run thing.

To the east of Utrecht the Dutch were forced back to positions almost on the outskirts of the city, but here they held firm. It was in Rotterdam that the issue was to be settled. Hitler was irritated that the Dutch had proved to be a harder nut to crack than he anticipated. He now gave orders that the matter be brought to a swift conclusion and on the morning of Tuesday 14 May General Winkelman received a message threatening the bombing of Rotterdam and Utrecht if resistance continued.

In Rotterdam itself the Germans had passed an eventful weekend. The record left by the soldier quoted above continues:

'11 May – Now the 9th Company is in front again. They have 45 men. We have only about 30. We are asking

LEFT **German forces at Tilburg, 14 May.** (B90/2/36A)

BELOW **A Dutch soldier carrying a flag of truce talks to German infantrymen.**

(Boersma)

ourselves if we will ever see our fatherland again! If we don't get reinforcements it's all over! At least we still have a couple of machine guns. We have lost … all anti-tank weapons… W., with his pack tied to his foot, crawled over the bridge on his stomach and bandaged the wounded …

'*13 May – During the night volunteers of the 16th Regiment) made their way across the bridge … Rope under the bridge, along which ammunition and provisions, with help of pulleys. Constant firing from enemy artillery … When are our tanks coming?*'

On Tuesday 14 May, on the southern edge of Rotterdam, the Germans were preparing for a decisive attack. They organised themselves in three groups, the first, Group A, consisted of tanks from Panzer Regiment 33 and the 3rd Battalion of Infantry Regiment 16, supported by artillery and engineers. They were to make a dash across the bridges to develop the bridgehead on the northern bank and advance towards Amsterdam. They would be followed by Group C, consisting of more tanks from Panzer Regiment 33 and the larger part of Leibstandarte SS-'Adolf Hitler' ordered to push north-west to relieve the paratroops beset by the Dutch at Oveschie on the Delft road. Group B, infantry from Regiment 33 and engineers, were to cross the Maas in barges near the confluence with the IJssel east of the bridges and push up into Kralingen, where the autoroute bridge now spans the river. As overtures for a Dutch surrender began, they were poised to move.

The message demanding surrender and threatening an air raid was sent to Colonel P. Scharroo, the officer commanding in Rotterdam, at his headquarters at 147 Statenweg. The opportunity to capitulate expired at 2.10 p.m. At that time the Germans were operating on their own time, that is, Greenwich Mean Time plus two hours. Britain, France and Belgium were all on GMT plus one hour, but the Dutch were still operating on GMT plus 20 minutes, so in their perception the ultimatum was to expire at 12.30 p.m., but it is not clear to what extent anyone really knew what the timing was meant to be. Scharroo telephoned Winkelman who demanded that

the Colonel seek clarification of the provenance of the message, so Captain Jan Backer was sent off under a flag of truce to the ice-cream parlour at 66 Prins Hendrikkade where Generalleutnant Rudolf Schmidt, commander of XXXIX Army Corps, had just arrived. He countersigned the offer and extended the time limit to 6 p.m. (4.20 p.m.), and simply required Dutch surrender and access to north Rotterdam by his troops. No mention was made in this document of bombing, for Schmidt had come to the conclusion that a cessation of hostilities was in negotiation and had sent a order to call off the raid. The bombers, however, were already airborne and observing radio silence.

The Heinkel He 111s were given the triangle of the city centre north of the bridges as their target, but were also instructed to look out for red flares which were to mark the positions of their own troops. Flares in the target area were to cancel the operation. The formation approaching from the south-east, 36 aircraft, saw the flares and most turned away, but the 56 machines coming from the east did not see any signal and dropped their full load. Some 97 tons of bombs fell on central Rotterdam, killing about

900 people. Colonel Scharroo went immediately to see Schmidt at Prins Hendrikkade and sign the surrender, protesting at the same time the needless loss of civilian lives.

At 3.30 in the afternoon surgeon C. van Staveren was dealing with a flood of civilian casualties at the Bergweg hospital when he was interrupted by one of his staff. Here, he said, was General Student. Staveren turned to see a figure on a stretcher, covered in blood, his head smashed and brain tissue exposed, but still conscious. He had been hit on the head, so the surgeon was told, by a falling beam when the command post on Statenweg was hit by a shell. Supervised by armed German medical orderlies, Staveren operated. The temptation to make a fatal mistake was almost overwhelming, but his integrity as a surgeon won over his human desire for revenge on the man who had reduced his city to ashes. Student's recovery was slow but complete and when visited by the surgeon he repeatedly mumbled 'You saved my life, you saved my life.' To Staveren it was a rebuke.

In Student's absence the final surrender of all Dutch forces was signed on 15 May by General Winkelman and General von Küchler at Student's

RIGHT **The memorial to the fallen at the Marinevliegkamp, Valkenburg.** (Audivisuelle-Dienst Kon. Marine, A9402-378)

BELOW **Graves of the fallen Dutch at Crooswijk Military Cemetery.** (Photo Amina Marix Evans)

BELOW RIGHT **Memorial to the Dutch surrender of 15 May outside the former school building at 101 Rijksstraatweg in Rijswoord.** (Photo Amina Marix Evans)

headquarters, a school in Rijsoord, south-east of Rotterdam.

Many of the Dutch commanders were angry and incredulous. They had not, they felt, been defeated, but they were ill-informed about the situation as a whole. Many naval units escaped for England, and the forces in Zeeland held on, together with the French, for some days. The Breda variation on Plan D was, however, over and the French were given orders to withdraw in support of Brussels. The Germans had expected only token resistance in the Netherlands and found instead that they had a real fight on their hands. None the less, in only five days it was over. The Dutch army had suffered 2,157 men killed while the Air Force had lost 75 and the Navy 125 men. Civilian deaths numbered 2,559 men, women and children. The figures seem small compared to those recorded for other countries later in the war, but the sacrifice of the slain was none the less just because they were few.

THE STRIKE INTO BELGIUM

The Belgian defences had, since 1936 when King Leopold declared neutrality, developed without liaison with their French or Dutch neighbours. When France started the Maginot Line in 1930, interest in building similar forts in Belgium was aroused, but the strategic concept for their organisation was ill-defined. Some wished to preserve the integrity of Belgian soil, others were for sacrificing immediate control of some territory in order to present the invader with a decisive mass of soldiery. Common to both approaches was the idea of the 'organised battlefield' – a space in which the enemy could be corralled and destroyed. Unfortunately it demanded a degree of co-operation from an adversary that was not forthcoming.

In the early 20th century great forts protected major cities such as Liège and Namur. These were overcome by the unexpected power of German artillery in 1914. Four yet more powerful forts were constructed and 15 old ones refurbished to create the Position Fortifiée de Liège (PFL) and the Position Fortifiée de Namur (PFN), while the PFA was arranged around Antwerp by transforming 27 forts into infantry strong-points. Lines of pillboxes and anti-tank ditches ran along the Albert Canal (which had been dug with the spoil piled on the southern side in the 1930s) from Antwerp south-eastwards in front of Maastricht to the PFL at Liège and then along the Maas (Meuse)

RIGHT **From Eben-Emael above the Albert Canal, the Maas is overlooked to the south-east.** (B751/96/27A)

south-west to Namur. Forward of that line the Stelling Grens was a curtain of some 400 pillboxes closer to the border. A puny line of pillboxes stretched tentatively towards France along the Meuse south of Namur. Within this defensive complex the Main Resistance Position included the PFA, the KW (Koningshooikt-Wavre) line and the PFN The KW line was created in 1939-1940 to provide the Dyle position envisaged by Plan D and the northern section was furnished with pillboxes and anti-tank fences. South of Wavre as far as Namur there were only fences and, by May 1940, it was still little more than an idea. Skimpy lines of pillboxes gave some cover to the Ardennes, but the strategy was based on the abandonment of that region should the Germans attack. The policy of neutrality also gave rise to the Ninove-Waterloo Position, a line of 55 pillboxes facing France, south of Brussels. As only 25 miles (40km) of anti-tank ditches and 125 miles (200 km) of anti-tank fencing had been completed by 1940, the defences were anything but continuous. The out-dated concept of the continuous defence line was itself invalidated by incomplete works.

The jewel in the crown of the system was the vast new fort of Eben-Emael, overlooking the Albert Canal. It was at the northern end of the new ring of forts around Liège (PFL) which continued with Aubin-Neufchâteau, Battice (the keystone of the complex) and Tancremont-Pepinster. It was armed with two 120mm and 16 75mm guns in great steel turrets and concrete casemates, as well as numerous machine-guns, and could cover approaches through Maastricht attempting to outflank the northern end of the PFL as well as offer supporting fire to Fort Neufchâteau. On the side close to the Albert Canal 60mm anti-tank guns supplemented

ABOVE **The 120mm gun turret in the centre of Eben Emael, the scar of a hollow charge can just be seen.** (Bernard Vrijens)

LEFT **German soldiers carrying 50 kg hollow charges at Fort Aubin-Neufchâteau** (Coll. Franck Vernier)

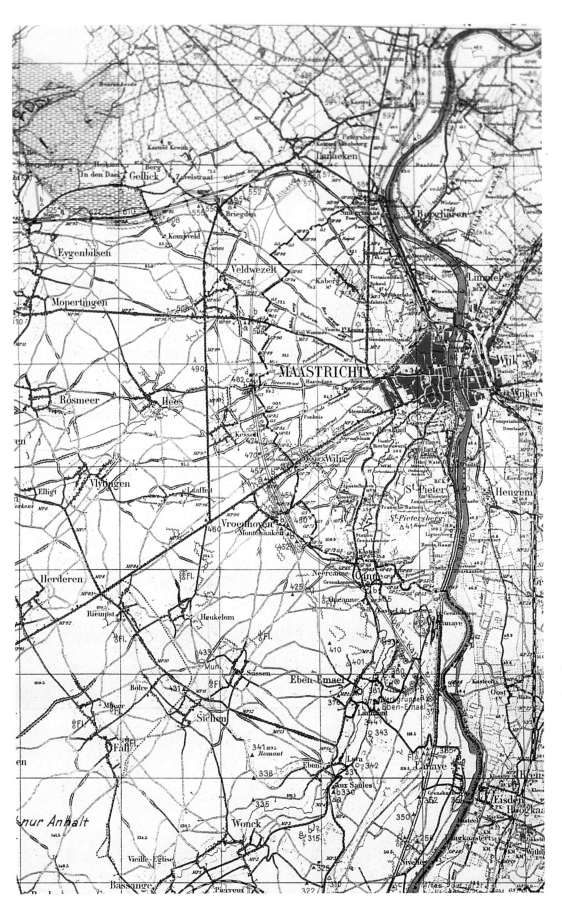

LEFT **The German map of the Belgian defences around Maastricht –** *Befestigungskarte Niederlande* **– dated 15 November 1939. Eben-Emael stands near the junction of the Albert Canal and the Maas, south of Maastricht.** (BL C29(21C), MME WW2/0/24)

RIGHT **Key to the German map of Belgian defences.** (MME WW2/0/26)

the machine-guns. The garrison numbered 1,400 men. The German armoured attack, aiming for the Gembloux gap halfway between Wavre and Namur, had to pass through the appendix of Dutch territory in which Maastricht stands, and thus had to undertake the flanking movement the fort was designed to prevent. Clearly it had to be neutralised. On 10 May 1940 it was.

ON SILENT WINGS

The seizure of the Albert Canal crossings was a task given to a special detachment under the command of Hauptmann W. Koch made up of men of Fallschirm-Jäger Regiment 1 and a platoon of engineers under Oberleutnant Rudolf Witzig. They had been given detailed and intensive training, isolated from family and comrades, for an attack on an unnamed objective. As evening approached on 9 May they learnt what it was. They were organised in four groups, to be carried by glider to swoop on their targets early the next day. Sturmgruppe Stahl (Steel) was to take the bridge over the canal near Veldwezelt, west-north-west of Maastricht, Group Concrete the bridge

ABOVE **A 60mm anti-tank gun, probably the best in the world in May 1940, at Fort Battice** (Coll. Franck Vernier)

LEFT **Fort Liezele, between Puurs and Breedonk, south-west of Antwerp, was completed in 1913 to supplement the early 19th century defences of the seaport. It was not taken by the Germans in 1914, but yielded as part of the general surrender. It was armed with machine guns in 1939-40.** (Photo Bart van Bulck)

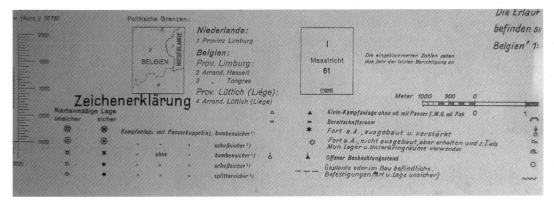

ABOVE **The heroes of the
attack, decorated with the
Knight's Cross by Adolf Hitler.
From the left, Delica, Witzig,
Koch, Zierach, Ringler,
Meissner, Kiess, Altmann and
Jäger.** (B74/113/13)

RIGHT **German troops cross a
makeshift bridge at
Maastricht.** (Boersma)

at Vroenhoven, further south, Iron the bridge at Canne and, at the southern end of the sector of operations, Group Granite, commanded by Witzig, was to attack the fortress of Eben Emael and hold it until Pioneer Battalion 51 and Infantry Regiment 151 could arrive to relieve them and hold the position.

At 4.15 a.m. on Friday 10 May Group Concrete, under Leutnant Gerhadt Schacht landed from ten gliders, one having broken its tow-line. Half an hour later Hauptman Koch flew in to set up his command post. The bridge was taken, but the Belgian 18th Regiment of the Line fought back and held the invaders to their confined positions until the next day. At Veldwezelt the Belgian 2nd Carabiniers opened fire at 4.20 a.m., bringing down one of the gliders, but fifteen minutes later the Germans had taken their objective. In the morning four Belgian T-13 tanks approached, but two of them were knocked out by anti-tank rifle fire and the others withdrew. Late in the day elements of the French 3rd Light Mechanised Division reconnoitred the position but by that time 4 Panzer had managed to come up and take over. The bridge at Canne was blown by the Belgian 2nd Grenadiers as Group Iron attacked, but the bridgehead was held until the German infantry came up in the afternoon.

Group Granite's approach started badly when one of the Ju 52s had to take evasive action to avoid another aircraft and its towed glider. The glider carrying the commander, Rudolf Witzig, crashed. The remaining gliders lost another of their number before reaching the objective, and thus only nine came hissing out of the darkness at 4.20 a.m. to land on top of Eben Emael. The Germans set about the turrets immediately with explosive charges. They had 83 *Geballte Ladung 3 kg.* which were conventional demolition charges that could also be used as satchel or pole charges, but more interesting were their

Hohlladung or hollow charges, of which they had 26 of 12.5kg. and 28 of 50 kg. These attempted to make use of the Monroe Effect which focused the forces released by the explosive in the direction of the hollow in a block of TNT. Later these would be developed to a state in which a fierce, narrow flame burned a hole through the target, but the primitive beehive versions available in 1940 used brute force, the effects of which can be seen to this day on the turrets of the fortress. A 12.5kg. charge blew a gun back into its casemate, and a 50kg. charge on the observation dome killed two men within. It was followed by grenades dropped through the hole which killed two more men. Germans spread from the other gliders to attack casemates, turrets and observation points with remarkable success. The retractable turret, *Coupole Sud*, rose in spite of a 50kg. charge being detonated on it and swept the surface of the fort with fire from its twin 75mm guns. Oberleutnant Witzig arrived at 7.30 a.m. after improvising an airstrip and calling up a replacement tow aircraft. Stukas were called in to deal with Coupole Sud which was forced to retract. Witzig then had his men take the fight inside the fort, but before they could penetrate the entrances Belgian troops were making their way up the north-western slopes and the Germans had to defend their gains. Meanwhile the forts of Barchon and Pontisse shelled the surface of Eben Emael. The Belgian attacks of 12.30 p.m. and 5 p.m. failed and at 8 p.m. the Belgians withdrew. During the night the Germans renewed their attacks and men of Infantry Regiment

151 crossed the Albert Canal in rubber boats to attack the north block with flame-throwers and 50kg. charges. Within the fort the garrison were in favour of surrender, but their commander, Major J. Jottrand, tried to rally them to fresh efforts. It was clearly hopeless. Shortly after noon on 11 May Eben Emael was surrendered. The last resistance on the Albert Canal was over.

To the east the bridges at Maastricht had been blown, but not entirely destroyed. Infantry were picking their way across the ruins and a makeshift footbridge supported by rubber boats. By 3.30 a.m. on Saturday 11 May engineers of 4 Panzer were ferrying men and light vehicles across the Maas on pontoons. By 4.30 a.m. the first pontoon bridge, a 16 ton-carrying structure capable of taking a tank, was operational. The Panzers were on the loose in Belgium.

Allied air response was attempted. Records and reports of the successive actions are contradictory and confusing, but it appears that Air Marshal Barratt ordered the Blenheims of 114 Squadron, based at Conde Vraux, near Soissons, to stand by and the aircraft were fuelled and bombed-up, ready to go when nine Dornier 17s of II/KG2 raced in, bombing and strafing. The squadron was destroyed. As daylight strengthened on the morning of Saturday, 11 May, nine Fairey Battles of the 5th Squadron, Belgian 3rd Group, took off to attack the German-held bridges. The anti-aircraft guns were already in position and the lumbering Battles were easy targets. Six of the aircraft survived long enough to press home the attack but

ABOVE **British troops entering Belgium, passing through Herseaux, east of Tourcoing, 10 May 1940.** (IWM F4335)

RIGHT **A French Hotchkiss H35/39 receives an enthusiastic welcome to Belgium.** (TM2433/D/2)

ABOVE **On the road from Tongres to Waremme, a light machine-gun troop of the 33rd Schützen (carrier borne) Regiment moves into the fields.** (B96/16/4A)

BELOW **Wrecked Belgian equipment, including a 4.7mm FRC gun, near Louvain, May 1940.** (TM 5787/A1)

alive with rumours, the best one being that Divisional Headquarters is surrounded by enraged German parachutists. So far we do not know why they are enraged!'

And again on Wednesday, 15 May, he reported:

'Today we had our usual parachute scare and were warned that the Germans might adopt any type of disguise including that of priests so when we saw 80 priests advancing down the road we felt confident we had caught a large contingent of them. We surrounded them and covered them from every possible angle and with every possible weapon; we then followed them into a wood. I myself, revolver in hand, advanced into the wood debating how many of them I would shoot before they shot me. I crept softly in and there came upon them on their knees giving thanks to God for having let them escape from the inferno behind them. I turned and came softly out feeling rather like a murderer must when viewing his unsuspecting victim.'

THE BATTLE OF THE GEMBLOUX GAP

The French First Army under General Blanchard and the Cavalry Corps under General René Prioux were south of the BEF, holding a line between Warve and the valley of the Meuse (Maas) river. Today the autoroute takes advantage of the flat, easy, rather dull country alongside the deep river valley and the hills of the western Ardennes. In 1940 the French saw it as the perfect route for the Panzers to sweep forward and the Germans were eager to behave in such a way as to convince the Allies that this was, indeed, their principal axis of attack. The vehicles of the 3rd and 4th Panzer Divisions poured over the Maastricht crossings and gathered themselves for action.

On the afternoon of Sunday, 12 May, Lieutenant Robert Le Bel, 3rd DLM looked from the turret of his Hotchkiss H-39, near Jandrain, to see:

'... an extraordinary show which was played out about three kilometres [2 miles] away: a panzer division shaping itself for battle. The massive gathering of this armoured armada was an unforgettable sight, the more so that it appeared even more terrifying through the glasses... Some men, probably officers, walked to and fro gesticulating in front of the tanks. They were probably giving last-minute orders ... Suddenly, as if swept away by a magic wand, they all disappeared... A dust cloud soon appeared on the skyline, disclosing the enemy move. I got down into the tank, closed the hatch and peered through the episcopes.'

The battle continued through the afternoon and into the evening. By nightfall the French had lost 24 Hotchkiss H-39s and four Somua S-35s, and the German losses caused them to remark on the bitter resistance offered by the French, necessitating repeated attacks by VIII Air Corps. The town of Hannut had fallen to the Germans. The next day, late in the morning, the Stukas were present in yet greater force. The French prevented the Germans from taking Merderop and, when the attackers tried to circumvent it, themselves launched an attack on the enemy's supporting infantry. In the close action that followed 4th Panzer no doubt enjoyed the advantages of their better radio communications. By the end of the day they were in Ramilles, 6 miles (10km) west of Hannut, and had inflicted the loss of 11 S-35s and four H-39s upon the 2nd Cuirassiers. To their north 3rd Panzer had pushed 1st Cuirassier back beyond Jauche and destroyed 25 of their tanks. Prioux was forced to order a withdrawal to a line east of the Wavre-Namur position.

The French infantry were now well established, so that when elements of 3rd Panzer slipped through the line in pursuit of 3rd DLM, they were comprehensively shot up by the 1st Moroccan Division. The battle resumed on 15 May between Gembloux and Perbaix, on both sides of Ernage and in confused fighting neither side had the upper hand, tanks and infantry attacking and counter-attacking. But now it was becoming clear to the Allies that the major stroke was falling elsewhere. The crossings of the Meuse to the south of the 1st Army, at Sedan on 13 May and Dinant on 14 May, threatened to outflank the Allies' Belgian positions. General Billotte ordered a retreat, first to a line on Waterloo and Charleroi, and then, on Thursday 16 May, to the river Escault from which they had started only six days earlier.

To the troops of the BEF, who had seen some shelling but little else, the orders came as a shock and to the Belgians it was a thunderbolt. Sysonby, who was in reserve on the Escault near Audenarde, said in a letter:

'The day before yesterday [Friday, 17 May] I was told at quarter to six p.m. to start a traffic control post at a cross-roads five miles [8km] away … By the time I got there portions of the Army had started pouring through. I can never describe to you the amazing scenes which took place. The inhabitants of the small village we were in were quite unprepared for this withdrawal and were completely stunned at the news that we were not advancing or even holding our ground… these wretched people had to leave, carrying everything in one suitcase and leaving their life's work and possessions behind them. All that day, all the next day and all last night the traffic never ceased pouring through.'

From the Dyle to the Senne, from the Senne to the Dendre and from the Dendre to the Escault the British fell back. The bridges were blown as they went. The artillery was in a constant state of redeployment as they, too, withdrew and took up positions to cover their comrades' withdrawal before moving to the rear again themselves. By Tuesday, May 21 the British had taken position on the Escault between Audenarde in the north, through Tournai to Maulde, halfway between Tournai and Valenciennes, there to stand against the Germans with the French First Army to their right and the Belgians to the north. Events elsewhere had already undermined this plan, as Lord Gort was becoming only too well aware.

BELOW **14 May 1940. As the British withdraw from Louvain the railway bridge is blown.** (IWM F4452)

THROUGH THE ARDENNES

The idea that the Ardenne terrain would not permit the passage of armoured forces has been used as an excuse for the lack of foresight of General Gamelin and his colleagues in the French High Command. That they were taken by surprise by the German attack is certain, but that they believed the Ardennes to be impenetrable to an army is incredible.

The description of the territory as 'impenetrable' has been attributed to Marshal Pétain who spoke of the Ardennes in March 1934, but went on to add 'provided we make some special dispositions.' In 1938 General Prételat was in command of manoeuvres that assumed an attack through the Ardennes of seven German divisions, four motorised infantry and with two tank brigades. The result was a defeat for the defenders of so comprehensive a nature that the wisdom of publishing it was questioned lest morale be

damaged. As late as March 1940 a French Deputy (member of Parliament) reported to Gamelin that the defences of Sedan were entirely inadequate. An attempt to increase the fortifications had been started the previous autumn, but the severe winter prevented the pouring of concrete and the delivery of the necessary materials. On 11 April General Huntzinger

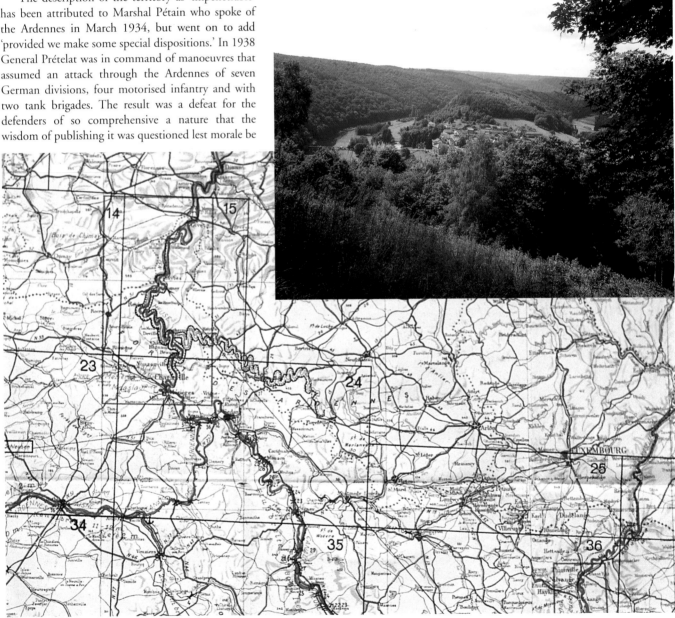

asked for another four divisions to work on the defences. He was refused. The history is thus not one of ignorance but of negligence.

From the high hills of the Eifel and Moselberg on the Belgian-German-Luxembourg borders, the land slopes away westwards, rolling country, wooded at first but opening up into broad, high fields. It is drained by the River Ourthe which runs north to join the Meuse at Liège, by the Lesse, heading north-west to Dinant, and the Semois which goes north-west almost parallel to the Meuse to its confluence with the larger river at Monthermé. The Meuse itself has cut deep into the landscape and the tributaries do the same. The impression is, indeed, of country difficult of access, surely wonderfully daunting for armoured divisions, but this is a superficial view. The eastern approaches to these valleys are relatively easy and the Meuse itself east of Charleville-Mézières runs through broad, welcoming country.

The handicaps the French imposed upon themselves on the ground were twofold. First, the Meuse itself was insufficiently fortified and, second, the Ardennes were left open in order to permit the French cavalry to advance. The impossibility of liaison with the Belgians contributed, for this was country they planned to abandon, but the lines of defence available above the Semois and along the Meuse were ignored with fatal results.

A further problem arose from the handling of intelligence. While the reconnaissance flights undertaken by the French Air Force were, they claimed, limited by their losses from enemy action and by the bad weather, the Deuxième Bureau provided French commanders with detailed information on the build-up of German troops, and the Swiss were aware of German bridge construction between Bonn and Bingen, as were the French. On 30 April the French Military Attaché in Berne reported that the Germans were to attack between 8 and 10 May with Sedan as the principal axis of the movement. These reports were, it must be remembered, a few amongst many that suggested the blow would fall elsewhere, but the facts of troop concentrations and bridge construction were not given proper weight against reports of mere plans.

ARMY GROUP A ADVANCES

The cutting edge of the German sickle was formed of the Panzer Corps of Rundstedt's Army Group A. On the right, in the Fourth Army heading for Dinant, was XV Panzer Corps under General Hermann Hoth, to whom Generalleutnant Max von Hartlieb (5th Panzer) and Generalmajor Erwin Rommel (7th Panzer) reported. Further south the Panzers of the Twelfth and Sixteenth armies were under the command of General Ewald von Kleist in a formation known as Gruppe von Kleist. The XLI Panzer Corps, commanded by General Georg-Hans Reinhardt, consisted of 6th and 8th Panzer, while XIX Panzer Corps, commanded by General Heinz Guderian,

MAP OPPOSITE **Detail from the February 1940 Generalstab des Heeres map *Gewässerabschnitte Nordost-Frankreich* which shows waterways and their crossing places. Dinant is top left, the Semois is shown flowing between high cliffs to join the Meuse at Monthermé in square 14 and Bouillon, hard to read, is top centre of square 24. Bertrix, Neufchâteau and Martelange are above square 24. The shading shows that a good deal of the country is fairly flat.** (MME WW2Maps/2/3)

PICTURE OPPOSITE **The village of Frahan on the River Semois, a scene thought typical of the Ardennes, contributing to the idea that the terrain was impenetrable.** (MME WW2/5/24)

LEFT **The terrain north-east of Bastogne; by no means impassable as events in 1944/45 would show once again.** (Photo David Playne)

ABOVE **German cavalry crosses the shallow Semois at Mouzaive, north-west of Bouillon.** (B84/68/23A)

BELOW **The village of Mouzaive, reached by a footbridge over the Semois.** (MME WW2/5/22)

comprised 1st, 2nd and 10th Panzer divisions and the Grossdeutschland Regiment, motorised infantry. Early in the afternoon of 9 May they were alerted to the coming action and, at 5.30 a.m. the next day, Guderian crossed the Luxembourg frontier at Wallendorf with 1st Panzer, heading for Martleange on the Belgian border, south of Bastogne.

They had been preceded by groups tasked with securing the southern flank. Oberleutnant Werner Hedderich's Luftlandekommando made swift and efficient work of securing key crossroads and easing the advance of the 34th Infantry Division into Luxembourg. The missions to seize positions at Nives and Witry, west of Martelange, went badly astray. The men involved were volunteers from the Grossdeutschland Regiment, 400 of them, who were to be flown in two-by-two, like Noah's cargo, in 100 Fieseler Fi 156 light aircraft. The pilots would have to

make two trips to deliver the force and in the event navigational errors and accidents led to some ending up yet further south at Léglise and all of them fairly scattered. A number of minor actions were fought with the Belgian 1st Chasseurs Ardennais and with elements of the French 5th Light Cavalry Division (DLC), some roads were blocked with felled trees and telephone lines cut. As the allied forces were under orders to withdraw and with the arrival of 2nd Panzer next morning, this venture quietly closed.

Guderian, meanwhile, had been troubled by the efficiency with which the Belgians had blocked the roads on the border. But they had, for the most part, withdrawn, leaving obstacles that, with a little time and effort, could be removed. The Germans were on the move again on the morning of Saturday 11 May, but matters had been confused by an order from Kleist's HQ for 10th Panzer to turn south to fend off a counter-attack by the French. Guderian succeeded in having this instruction withdrawn, but the 10th were now in the sector of advance planned for 1st Panzer which, in turn, got in the way of the 2nd which then interfered with 6th Panzer. Fortunately for the Germans, the sky was innocent of allied bombers to attack the traffic jams. Neufchâteau was defended by Belgian Chasseurs Ardennais and French 3rd Spahis and 5th DLC, but a brisk fight supported by Stukas drove them off both here and at Bertrix. By night 1st Panzer had reached the outskirts of Bouillon on the Semois, only 10 miles (15km) from Sedan. The bridge here had been blown, as had the bridge at the tobacco-growing village of Frehan to the west. During the night elements of the reconnaissance battalion crept over the ford at Mouzaive, further west again, and established themselves south of the Semois. Also during this night GRII/33, the French strategic reconnaissance squadron, observed routes in the Belgian Ardennes thronged with blazing headlights as the invaders hastened towards the Meuse. Their report appears to have been ignored.

To the north Rommel had had less difficulty in advancing. He wrote:

'All roads and forest tracks had been permanently barricaded and deep craters blown in the main roads. But most of the road blocks were undefended by the Belgians, and it was thus in only a few places that my division was held up for any length of time. Many of the blocks could be by-passed by moving across country or over side roads...

'At our first clash with French mechanised forces, prompt opening fire on our part led to a hasty French retreat. I have found again and again that in encounter actions, the day goes to the side that is the first to plaster its opponent with fire... this applies even when the exact position of the enemy is unknown, in which case the fire must simply be sprayed over enemy-held territory.'

On the morning of Whit Sunday, 12 May, Guderian drove to Bouillon where he was able to congratulate Lieutenant-colonel Hermann Balck on the taking of the town by his 1st Rifle Regiment at about 8 a.m. After checking the progress of 10th Panzer further east where they had crossed the Semois between Cugnon and Herbeumont, he returned to the headquarters his Chief of Staff, Colonel Nehring, had set up on the Hôtel Panorama. They were just getting down to work when:

'Suddenly there was a series of explosions in rapid succession; another air attack… the fine window in front of which I was seated was smashed to smithereens and splinters of glass whistled about my ears.'

They decided to move and eventually settled north of Noirefontaine. This time the Battles of the AASF had attacked and returned unscathed, although the bridge-building at Bouillon continued undisturbed; in the afternoon half of the 12 aircraft attacking the German column further north were lost.

Guderian's adventures were not over for the day. A Fieseler Storch aircraft was sent to take him to Kleist's headquarters, where he learned that the crossing of the Meuse was scheduled for 4 p.m. the next day and that a mass bombing rather than the close support attacks of the Stukas was planned. Guderian argued against this, but was over-ruled. Then, for the second time in a day, he was in danger. On the return trip the pilot got lost. To his alarm the General discovered that they were flying along, in an unarmed aircraft, on the southern side of the Meuse. An immediate order to turn north was issued! Once more in his headquarters, Guderian considered the task of drawing up orders for the next day.

'In view of the very short time at our disposal, we were forced to take the orders used in the war games at Koblenz from our files and, after changing dates and time, issue these as orders for the attack. They were perfectly fitted to the situation… 1st and 10th Panzer copied this procedure …'

OVER THE MEUSE: SEDAN

On the morning of Monday, 13 May, General Pierre Grandsard, commander of X Corps, the left wing of Huntzinger's 2nd Army, asserted that nothing new would happen for a few days while the Germans brought up their heavy artillery and ammunition supplies. At 11 a.m. the Luftwaffe started an immense air raid, pounding French fortifications with Stukas, Dorniers and Heinkels. Some 500 sorties were flown. Cowering under this torrent were the reservists of the 55th Infantry Division, one of France's weaker formations. The other division that made up X Corps, the 71st, had been ordered forward during the night but was not yet in position. French artillery fire was limited as there was a fear of running out of ammunition. The Germans were able to push tanks forward to the river and fire on the French pillboxes, many of them unfinished and not even equipped with doors. The 88mm anti-aircraft gun was also able to do substantial harm to French installations. Men crept forward with rubber boats, ready to attempt the crossing. The aerial bombardment culminated in precisely the concentrated dive-bomber attack Guderian wanted – General Lörzer had contrived to leave the original plan for 4 p.m. in place.

LEFT **Men of Rommel's 7th Panzer deal with trees felled across the roads by the Belgians.** (IWM RML52)

ABOVE **The town of Bouillon and the river seen from the medieval castle.** (MME WW2/5/30)

The crossings took place on both sides of Sedan. At Glaire 1st Panzer managed to cross from the shelter of the factory south-west of Floing and 10th Panzer crossed at Wadelincourt, but at Donchery 2nd Panzer were brought under heavy fire and failed. Guderian hastened to Floing and crossed in an assault boat to Glaire where he found Lieutenant-colonel Balck:

'He greeted me cheerfully with the cry: 'Joy riding in canoes on the Meuse is forbidden!' I had in fact used those words myself in one of the exercises that we had in preparation for this operation, since the attitude of some of the younger officers had struck me as rather too light-hearted. I now realised that they had judged the situation correctly.'

Guderian goes on to report that their covering fire had been very effective and their casualties light. By 11.30 p.m. they had pushed up the ridge to the south as far as Cheveugues and taken part of the Bois de la Marfée. Donchery was now in 2nd Panzer's hands. Work on a pontoon bridge at Glaire was progressing and 1st Panzer's tanks were over as the new day

LEFT **From the D205 running south-west from Illy, the village of Floing is seen below, left, and Donchery beyond and to the right. On the other side of the valley of the Meuse the hills rise steeply to the Bois de la Marfée.** (MME WW2/5/34)

dawned. French resistance had crumbled away and reinforcing units found themselves obstructed in their advance by fleeing comrades.

By midnight, the end of Monday 13 May, three pontoon bridges, at Donchery, Glaire and Wadelincourt, were carrying heavy traffic to the south bank. The 1st and 2nd Panzer were well down the road alongside the River Bar and the Canal des Ardennes. Guderian reflected to himself that the success of his attack was almost a miracle.

THE MEUSE AT DINANT

By Sunday, 12 May, it was dawning on General Corap that his Ninth Army was getting involved in something serious. He issued an order stating that it was crucial to throw back any German force that set foot on the west bank of the Meuse. He was a little slow off the mark. He pulled the 1st and 4th Light Cavalry back over the Meuse and tried to hasten the 18th and 22nd Infantry to the defence, but they, third-grade troops below strength in any case, were coming up on foot. With the best will in the world, they could go no faster.

On the afternoon of that day the leading elements of Rommel's 7th Panzer had reached the Meuse at Dinant in time to see the bridge blown at 4.20 p.m. The neighbouring bridges at Bouvignes and Anseremme went at much the same time. To the north the railway bridge at Houx had gone earlier in the afternoon, but the bridge at Yvoir was kept open to the last minute as the Belgians were still falling back. As Kampfegruppe Werner, a 5th Panzer unit temporarily under 7th Panzer command, approached the bridge the electrical demolition circuit was closed. Nothing

ABOVE **A Stuka dive-bomber. This is a JU87B-2.** (John Weal, *Junkers Ju 87 Stukageschwader 1937-41, Osprey Combat Aircraft 1*)

MAIN PICTURE **The village of Bazeilles seen from Pont Maugis, south of the river, where a bunker stands in a peaceful field.** (MME WW2/5/37)

happened. Lieutenant René De Wispelaere of the Belgian 31st Engineers Battalion ran forward and shortened the time-fuse of the non-electrical back-up system to virtually nothing and ignited it. As he turned to run back he was shot. The bridge went up with the first German vehicles on it.

The remaining bridges up and down stream were destroyed later in the day, leaving rubber boats and pontoons as the obvious means of crossing. It gave a little more time for the French to gather their strength. The German 7th Motor-cycle Battalion approached the river at Houx by way of Awagne, sending out a reconnaissance patrol from that village at 5 p.m. They found the railway bridge gone, but saw that a weir

ABOVE **First Panzer Regiment approach Bouillon, 13 May.** (B88/112/19)

RIGHT **Guderian surveys the scene in Bouillon.** (B80/4/32)

OPPOSITE TOP **An 88mm gun in field artillery mode.** (B400/182/14)

OPPOSITE BOTTOM **Detail from German 1:25,000 mapping of France showing Sedan centre right and, to the north-west, Glaire on the south bank and the factory across the Meuse to the east. The challenge of the hills south of the river can be appreciated.** (BL C21 (15) sheet XXX-9/7-8, MME WW2Maps/3/36)

between the east bank and an island appeared to be whole. The associated navigational lock was on the other side, overlooked by the French 2nd Battalion, 39th Infantry at Senenne and on the bank between the river and the railway. To their south the 1st/66th were scarcely in place forward of Rostenne. During the night the Germans crept forward and then, with covering fire from their machine-guns, made all speed across the old stone weir. The island was unoccupied. At 5.30 a.m. on Monday, 13 May, they pushed on over the lock and, in a hail of fire, established a small bridgehead. In rubber boats, with covering fire from tanks on the east bank, more men came over. As the dawn drew on to morning they took Grange and by noon held an area three miles (5km) square.

Early that Monday Rommel arrived in Dinant to find the 6th Rifle Regiment attempting to cross the river in boats but suffering severely from artillery and rifle fire from the Belgians and French. The crossing was stuck. He then checked Houx and told the 7th Motor-cycle to clean up and secure their bridgehead. South once more, he found the 7th Rifle Regiment with a company over the river at Bouvignes, but under fire too heavy to permit reinforcement. He wrote:

'As there was clearly no hope of getting any more men across at this point without powerful artillery and tank support to deal with enemy nests, I drove back to Division Headquarters, where I met the Army Commander, Colonel-General von Kluge and the Corps commander, General Hoth… I drove back along the Meuse to Leffe [immediately north of Dinant] to get the crossing moving there. I had already given orders for several Panzer IIIs and IVs and a troop of artillery to be at my disposal at the crossing point.'

The scene that greeted them was depressing; rubber boats lying damaged and the men under cover. The Leffe weir bridge had been barred with a spiked steel plate. Then the tanks Rommel had ordered up arrived as well as two howitzers. The Belgians and French were subjected to steady, well-aimed fire, German tanks driving along the east bank with turrets traversed to bring their 75mm guns to bear. The crossing started once more and Rommel went over to encourage his men forward. After a probing advance by French armoured vehicles, probably armoured cars, had been frightened off by small-arms fire under his orders, the General returned to the east bank and went up to Houx to push things forward there. He found the engineers building 8-ton pontoons, too light for tanks, and ordered them to get on with the 16-ton type to get the tanks across the river. Work went slowly, but there were 15 of them across by the next morning. It was as well, for a mixed force of French, infantry, Dragoons and a reconnaissance unit, ran into the Germans at Haut-le-Wastia, west of Anhée, and retreated only when tanks came up.

As Rommel exploited his bridgehead on the Tuesday morning by attacking Onhaye, up on the

plateau west of Dinant, where Colonel von Bismark's 7th Rifle Regiment had arrived, General Corap was making arrangements to oppose him. He ordered General Julien Martin of XI Corps to take command of 1st Armoured Division and 4th North African Infantry Division and make a counter-attack. The former was regrouping some nine miles (15km) west of Dinant and the latter had just completed long marches under Luftwaffe harassment.

The seizure of Onhaye on Tuesday, 14 May, did not go smoothly for Rommel. He rushed forward with what armour he had on the west bank under the impression that Bismark was surrounded, but found the message had been misunderstood. He then left Bismark commencing an encircling movement on the village. Rommel himself made for a wood to the north of the village to assemble his tanks there. Suddenly they came under fire.

'Shells landed all round us and my tank received two hits, one after the other, the first on the upper edge of the turret and the second in the periscope. The driver promptly opened the throttle wide and drove straight into the nearest bushes. He had only gone a few yards, however, when the tank slid down a steep slope … and stopped, canted over on its side, in such a position that the enemy … could not fail to see it.'

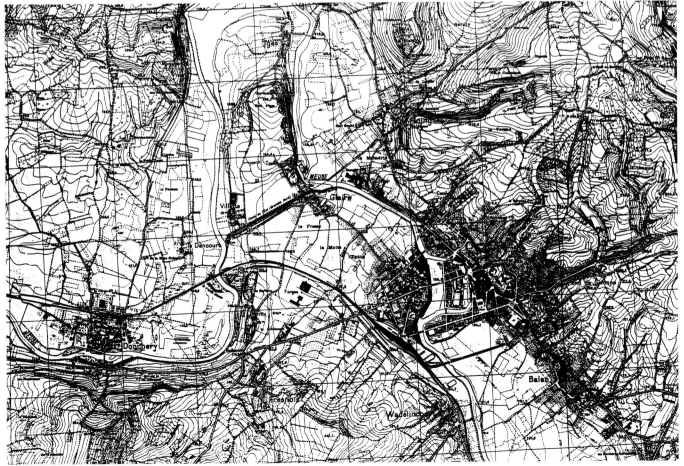

RIGHT **Rommel's crossing area on the Meuse. A road bridge was kept open between Yvoir and Anhée, at the north of the hour-glass shape made by roads and railway. The rail bridge south of this had been blown. The road east from Houx was the approach of 7th Panzer and the lock is at the south-western end of the island with the weir on the east.** (ICM, Brussels, 1940, sheet 53. MME WW2Maps/3/30)

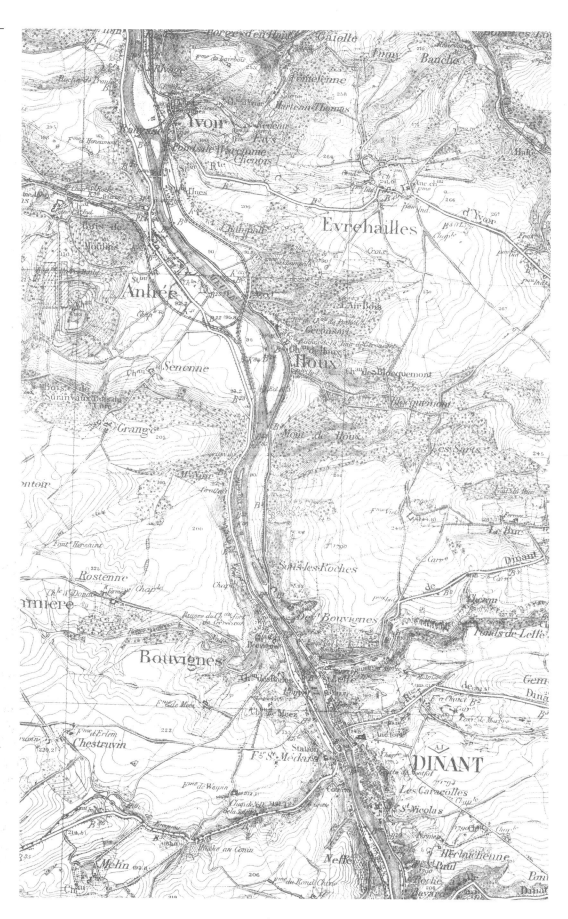

LEFT **Dinant, from the Château Crèvecourt above Bouvignes-sur-Meuse. The Fortress stands on the hill above the Collègiale, the church, with the road bridge below. Downstream is Leffe weir and lock. The bridge at Bouvignes was not rebuilt.** (MME WW2/7/16)

BELOW **The lock and weir at Houx, seen from the medieval village and Château de Poilvache on the hilltop to the north.** (MME WW2/7/23)

He decided to abandon the tank. The smoke candles on another Panzer had been ignited by the shellfire and, under the cover of the smoke-screen thus created, they managed to get to safety. Stukas were called up to deal with the artillery and a further attack in the evening gave Rommel the Onhaye position with the broad, open country before him.

MONTHERMÉ

General Reinhardt's XLI Panzer Corps had the most difficult approach to the Meuse given the combination of distance travelled and the narrow roads. The 6th Panzer Division was to cross at Monthermé while 8th Panzer went for Nouzonville to the south. The bridge at Monthermé was down and barbed wire and pillboxes could be seen on the far bank. Here, on Monday 13 May, the machine-gunners of the 42nd Demi-Brigade of Colonial Infantry, part of the 102nd Fortress Division, awaited them. Three companies of German infantry in rubber boats attempted the crossing. One was thrown back, but two managed to gain a foothold and fought stubbornly all day to secure a small bridgehead, wiping out the 5th Company of the 42nd Demi-Brigade in doing so. The French withdrew to their prepared positions at the foot of the peninsula. The Germans then managed to get men over the river on the ruins of the bridge to reinforce their position while a pontoon bridge was constructed

but it was not until Wednesday, 15 May, that, with the help of pressure from the flanks, 6th Panzer broke through the stubborn French resistance.

GUDERIAN'S RIGHT WHEEL

On the morning of Tuesday, 14 May, Guderian's 1st Panzer had advanced as far as Chéhéry, some four miles (7km) south of the Meuse, overlooking the River Bar and the Canal des Ardennes to the west. This waterway joins the Meuse a little over four miles west

ABOVE RIGHT **The memorial to René De Wispelaere near the new Anhée/Yvoir road bridge.** (MME WW2/7/17)

RIGHT **The confluence of the Meuse and the Semois (Semoy) at Monthermé. Detail from a map published by the German *Geographischen Dienst der Armee.*** (BL C21 (15) sheet XXX-8/5-6-7)

OPPOSITE TOP **The Meuse at Monthermé.** (MME WW2/5/9)

OPPOSITE MIDDLE **Deville, downstream of Monthermé, seen from a Panzer south of the village, two months after the crossing.** (B85/37/15A)

OPPOSITE BOTTOM **14 May 1940: the radio section of 9th Infantry Regiment in Aiglemont, south of, and high above, Nouzonville.** (B73/139/23)

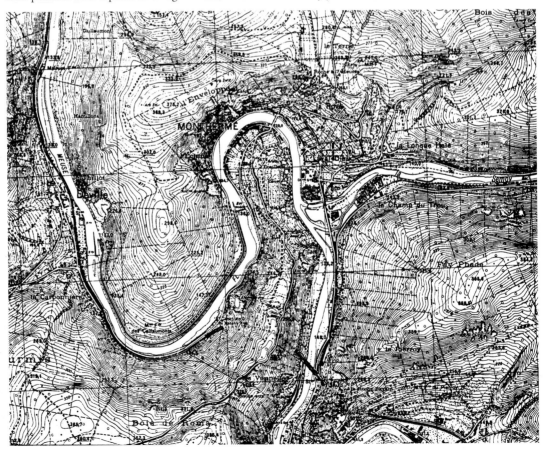

of Sedan and is the last stream until the Oise 60 miles (100km) to the west. Guderian's account gives the place as Chémery, but this is as far south again, and would have been fatally exposed to counter-attack. The bridge at Glaire was also bringing 2nd Panzer across, and they were moving west along the south bank of the Meuse.

The French were attempting to stem this tide. The previous afternoon had seen a panic on the south bank. French troops had reported seeing tanks at Bulson, south-east of Chéhéry, and both infantry and gunners had tumbled to the rear in a rabble. The commander of the 55th Division, General Lafontaine, withdrew his headquarters to Chémery and attempted to organise a counter-attack. Some men, such as Major Benedetti of the 363rd Regiment, managed to advance and engage the Germans, but the majority, dispirited and confused, did little or nothing. This permitted the Germans to reach Chéhéry unopposed. On the morning of 14 May it was intended to use two groups to push the Germans back, 4th Tank Battalion (Bataillon de Chars de Combat) and 205th Infantry on the right and 7th Tank Battalion and 213th Infantry, under Lieutenant-Colonel Labarthe, on the left. Only the latter was ready by 7 a.m., and so Labarthe alone was ordered to attack.

The tanks were FCM 36s, light tanks armed with obsolete 37mm guns, but well handled they could still give 1st Panzer problems, and at first they did, catching them refuelling and knocking out two tanks immediately. The Germans fought back furiously, holding 7th Tanks until their own armour could strike. At 8.30 a.m. they hit the 7th at Connage, leaving them with only three of their 13 tanks. An attack by the Grossdeutschland Regiment threw the French out of Bulson with the loss of another 19 tanks. The Germans hurried on to Chémery where they were hit by their own Stukas, suffering the loss of four dead and a number of wounded.

General Lafontaine decided not to risk the second attack group and the French fell back towards the ridge to the south. The French 3rd Armoured Division was moving up with two battalions on the road north from Le Chesne and two coming up through Stonne. Two infantry regiments were also available. A concentrated attack was possible. It was not made. Fearful of his ability to hold the Germans, General Jean Flavigny, commander of XXI Corps to which these forces belonged, decided they should be dispersed to stiffen a long line of defence rather than knock his opponents out, so scattered were they.

In the early hours of Tuesday, 14 May General Billotte telephoned Air Marshal Barratt for assistance and the AASF sent six Battles in to attack the pontoons at about 5 a.m. and another four at about 7.30 a.m. All returned safely and some hits on the bridges were reported, but the flow of Panzers to the

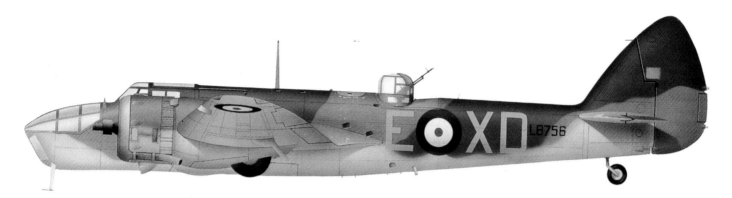

ABOVE **A Blenheim IV of 139
Squadron, Plivot, France, April
1940.** (Chris Davy, *Blenheim
Squadrons of World War 2*, Osprey
Combat Aircraft 5)

south bank seemed undiminished. The French
Air Force put in their first attack at 9 a.m., on
10th Panzer's sector at Douzy and Bazeilles, with eight
Breguet 693s protected by 15 RAF Hurricanes and 15
Bloch 152s. Later in the morning five LeO 451s and a
dozen obsolescent Amiot 143 night bombers were sent
against the bridges and troops at Sedan. Of those that
survived the mission none were airworthy. That
exhausted the French resources and the attacks were
taken up by the AASF Air Vice-Marshal Playfair had
62 Battles and eight Blenheims left and committed
them all. It spelt the end of his force. The Battles lost

35 of their number and the Blenheims five, while the
returning aircraft were badly shot up. Two of the
pontoon bridges were sunk (though they were quickly
replaced) and bridges at Mouzon and Sedan were hit.
As evening approached 28 Blenheims of 2 Group
attacked and a quarter of them were lost. Guderian
remarked:

*'There was now a most violent air attack by the
enemy. The extremely brave French and English pilots did
not succeed in knocking out the bridges, despite the heavy
casualties that they suffered. Our anti-aircraft gunners
proved themselves on this day, and shot superbly. By*

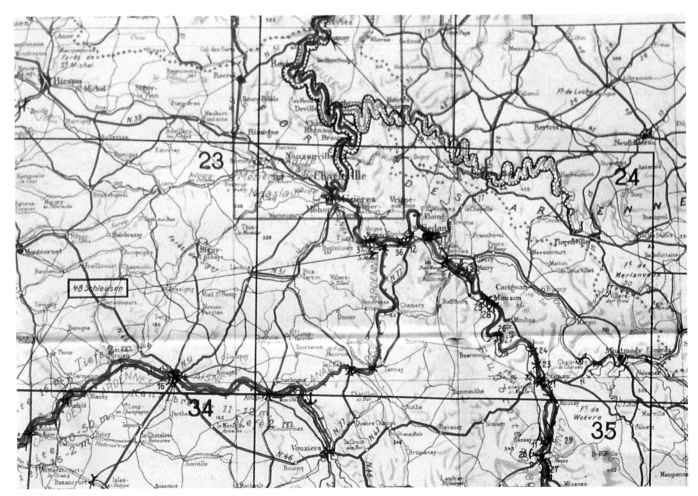

LEFT **Fallen British aircrew lie at Noyers-Pont Maugis alongside French infantrymen who died defending the Meuse line in May 1940.** (MME WW2/6/4)

BELOW LEFT **To the west from the Butte de Stonne, with the village to the left, the observer has a commanding view of the country Guderian had to cross.** (MME WW2/6/36)

MAP OPPOSITE **The area of the Meuse crossings in France, with the Canal des Ardennes running south. Stonne commands the exit from the wedge of land bordered east and west by the canal and the river. Detail from** *Gewässerabschnitte Nordost-Frankreich,* **Berlin, February 1940. Bridges are clearly shown.** (MME WW2Maps/2/30)

evening they calculated [over optimistically] that they had accounted for 150 enemy aeroplanes.'

The German ability swiftly to get the anti-aircraft guns established to defend their river crossings was demonstrated here as it was in Belgium.

KLOTZEN, NICHT KLECKERN

In the afternoon of 14 May Guderian was back with 1st Panzer, now in control of the road south at Chémery-sur-Bar. He asked General Kirchner if he felt the whole division should be turned west or if a south-facing flank guard should remain on the east side of the canal. A staff officer, Major Wenck, immediately remarked: 'Klotzen, nicht Kleckern' – Bash, don't tap. It was an expression Guderian himself used, meaning one should employ a concentrated force in a single blow, not spread the force over multiple strikes. It was apt. The whole division would turn.

The concern was that the Sedan bridgehead was overlooked by the hills running west to east through

ABOVE **On the southern side of the hilltop at Noyers-Pont Maugis German fallen of two World Wars are buried.** (MME WW2/6/10)

RIGHT **A Panzer IV destroyed in Stonne by 41st Tank Battalion on 16 May.** (B87/54/8)

Stonne, and would be insecure unless those heights were also in German hands. It was decided that 10th Panzer and the Grossdeutschland Regiment would take care of that. The infantry regiment was in Maisoncelle that afternoon and moved on to Artaise, but were unable to make further progress against unexpected fire from the French 6th Reconnaissance Group and 51st, 67th and 91st Infantry. From Wednesday, 15 May and for the next three days the ridge would be an inferno. The 10th Panzer attacked at dawn and lost a tank to 6th Recce at the Sugar Loaf (*Pain de Sucre*) hair-pin bend east of the village. The Grossdeutschland Regiment pressed and took Stonne, but the French 49th Tank Battalion advanced at about 7.30 a.m. with ten Renault B1bis under the command of Lieutenant Caraveo in the *Toulal*. They withdrew after the Germans had made themselves scarce, after which, at about 10 a.m., the Germans reoccupied

ABOVE LEFT **French Hotchkiss H-39s prepare to attack from cover.** (TM 2937/E2)

LEFT **The struggle to stay mobile – French Renault R35s in a field repair shop.** (TM KY7108)

Stonne. Caraveo returned to the attack and ran into heavy anti-tank fire, losing three of his company's vehicles, the *Hautvillers* which caught fire, the *Gaillac* which exploded and the *Chinon* which burnt out. These last two involved the loss of their crews as well. Three other tanks were damaged and the company withdrew to the southern edge of the village. Here they were united with the 45th Tank Battalion and the 67th Infantry to launch another counter-attack. To their left 51st Infantry attacked from the woods, supported by Hotchkiss H39s. The village was retaken, but could not be held that night when the supporting tanks had to withdraw. The Germans regained it. The village of Stonne was being reduced to ruins.

The morning of 16 May saw French artillery smash the rubble of Stonne into yet smaller fragments. Two companies of Renault B1bis of 41st Tank Battalion went in at 5 a.m. Captain Pierre Billotte in the tank *Eure* saw, as he reached the centre of the village, a column of panzers approaching. He immobilised the first of them, then,

'The panzers following it were spaced at regular intervals on a 200-metre climb, each of them being shielded by those in front. On the other hand, I was uphill and I could fire at them from above… In ten minutes, the panzers at the head of the column were all silenced, one after the other, and I could see the ones in the rear hastily withdrawing.'

Billotte then destroyed an anti-tank gun with the 75mm. The 41st had retaken the wreckage of Stonne. On Friday 17 May the Germans relieved 10th Panzer and the Grossdeutchland Regiment and threw their 2nd Infantry against the French. They suffered at the hands of the 49th Tank Battalion, but prevailed.

The French tanks were back the next day and, with the 51st Infantry, managed to get back into Stonne once more, only to be shelled out by the end of the day. The German infantry was catching up with Kleist's Panzer Group and the attackers now had three divisions to dedicate to acquiring the ridge. It was not until Friday 24 May that they could force the French to withdraw.

By then Guderian was far away. His 1st and 2nd Panzer Divisions had crossed the canal on Wednesday 15 May. Then, at La Horgne, ten miles (15km) west of Chémery, they were met by the 3rd Brigade of Spahis, the unit which had been pulled off the Semois prematurely a couple of days earlier. There was no such withdrawal now. For ten hours the 1st Cavalry Brigade and the Spahis, not merely a cavalry regiment in name but mounted on horses, held the Germans. The Spahis suffered 30% casualties before they finally fell back. The way to the west was clear.

It was nearly not so. The order had been given for a 24-hour halt to consolidate. Guderian wrote:

'I neither would nor could agree to these orders, which involved the sacrifice of the element of surprise we had gained and of the whole initial success we had achieved. I therefore got in touch, personally, first with the Chief of Staff of the Panzer Group, Colonel Zeitzler, and since this was not enough with General von Kleist himself, and requested that the order to stop be cancelled. The conversation became very heated and we repeated our various arguments several times. Finally, General von Kleist approved of the advance being continued for another twenty-four hours so that sufficient space be acquired for the infantry corps that were following... I was pleased to have retained my freedom of movement ...'

SICHELSCHNITT

Lieutenant Patrick Turnbull was serving with GHQ at Arras. On Monday 13 May, he was sent to inspect the damage resulting from an attack by the Luftwaffe on the railway station.

'I found there had been a number of direct hits on the station which was burning fiercely. One bomb had evidently fallen in the place [square] just outside the entrance near a group of children either returning from school or about to be put on a train to carry them further west to imagined safety. Six or seven mangled little bodies lay messily on the cobbles, blood spattering the gutters. Two nights later the Hotel Univers in turn suffered a direct hit. I arrived on the scene just in time to see the remains of an officer with whom I had been dining the previous evening being dragged from the rubble... Evidence that all was far from well was accumulating, but even by the 16th there was no impact of crisis. Perhaps it was that after so long a spell of wearisome phoney war, the increasing chaos seemed equally phoney.'

The lack of urgency infected the French High Command. General Georges had told Gamelin of a serious pin-prick at Sedan, but then reported that the Germans had been held. It was entirely false, though Georges evidently believed it. While Panzer Group Kleist launched itself westwards, the French 3rd Armoured Division was being destroyed piecemeal on the heights around Stonne. In the north the 1st Armoured had suffered a similar fate.

FLAVION TO LE CÂTEAU

General Marie-Germain Bruneau, in command of 1st Armoured Division, had some 160 to 180 tanks at his disposal; records are vague. Of these about 70 were Renault B1bis, with 28th and 37th Tank Battalions, and some 90 were Hotchkiss H39s with 25th and 26th Tanks. The division had originally been intended for the support of Plan D and on 11 May was sent to

ABOVE **Two of the eight Chars B of 3rd Company destroyed on 15 May by the Germans as the French moved north, leaving Denée to their right, seeking the main east-west road.** (TM 2438/L7)

LEFT **A Char B of 2 Company, 37th Tanks broken down in Ermeton-sur-Biert. The highly vulnerable radiator grille can clearly be seen.** (TM 2438/C5)

PONT DE LA 42ème
DEMI-BRIGADE DE
MITRAILLEURS
D'INFANTERIE COLONIALE
MAI 1940

LEFT **Monthermé, where the machine-gunners of the colonial infantry were overcome. The bridge bears a small plaque in their memory.**
(MME WW2/5/4 & 6)

BELOW **A dug-out entrance and, in the distance, a pillbox, west of Clairfayts, where Rommel claimed to have broken the Maginot Line.**
(MME WW2/4/32)

Charleroi in southern Belgium, ordered to travel by night to avoid air attack and allowed four nights to do it. Orders then changed, they had to go faster, use fewer nights, and they got there late on Sunday 12 May. On Monday they did nothing, in spite of the furore on the Meuse. General Corap then decided that he had to abandon the Meuse line and create a new defence further west, on a line through Philippeville. The confusion following on this decision was to make progress much easier for the Germans.

On Tuesday 14 May, as Rommel was attacking Onhaye, 1st Armoured was ordered to Florennes, 12 miles (20km) west of Dinant, and arrived there late that night, in some disorder and with the fuel trucks following at the very end of the column. Rommel had, by this time, taken Onhaye against the resistance of units of the 4th North African Division, Zouaves and Algerians. The Algerians fought alone, without co-ordination with their armoured troops, against 7th Panzer while the similarly isolated 39th and 66th Infantry, facing the Germans of 5th Panzer west of Houx, were mopped up as well, in spite of gallant resistance.

On the morning of Wednesday 15 May, the Renaults of 28th Tanks were at Flavion, just north of the main Dinant-Philippeville road and about nine miles (14km) from Dinant, with the Hotchkiss H39s of the 25th to their rear in Corenne. The rest of the Hotchkiss, with 26th, were to the north-east and beyond them, close to Ermeton-sur-Biert, were the other Chars B of the 37th. Leading tanks of 7th Panzer

were seen in Anthée, on the main road south-east of Flavion, at about 8.30 a.m. and fired on by the 28th. Rommel wrote of this day:

'My intention for the 15th May was to thrust straight through in one stride to our objective, with the 25th Panzer Regiment in the lead and with artillery and, if possible, dive-bomber support. The infantry was to follow up the tank attack, partly on foot and partly lorry-borne. The essential thing, to my mind, was that the artillery should curtain off both flanks of our attack ...'

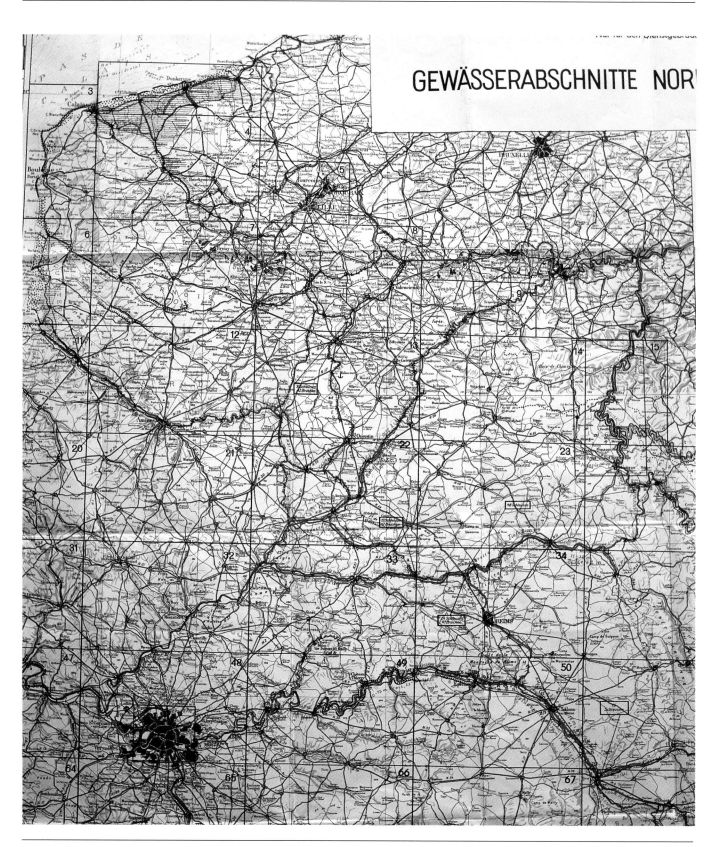

ABOVE **The routes to the English Channel suitable for AFVs and mechanised infantry support become evident on the German February 1939 Gewässerabschnitte map of North-west France. Rommel's path from Dinant (above square 15) was by Cambrai (square 13) and left around Arras (7) and up to Lille (5). Guderian went by Moncornet (23), St Quentin (22, top), Péronne (13) and Amiens (12) to the coast. The map gave considerable detail of the nature of the waterways and the bridges and fords over them, as well as showing doubtful ground. The hatched areas are below sea-level.** (MME WW2Maps MF2/3)

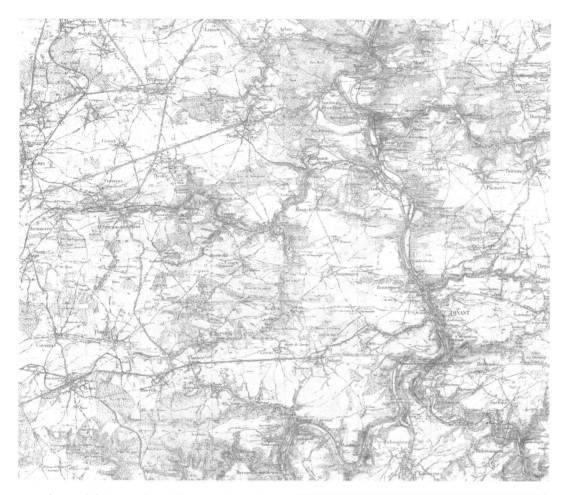

LEFT **The country west of the Meuse at Dinant. The Dinant-Philippeville road passes through Onhaye, Anthée and Rosée. The distance from Gerin to Rosée is approximately six miles (10km). The tank action on 15 May was fought to the north of this road.** (From ICM, Brussels, 1940, sheet 53. MME WW2Maps MF2/15)

BELOW **At the junction of the Rue Haute (D104) and the unclassified Rue de Willies, west of Clairfayts, a house carries the memorial to the 84th Regiment of Infantry.** (MME WW2/4/34)

A better definition of a sickle-stroke is hard to imagine. When the French fired on Rommel's leading tanks, they took to the woods and kept going west, avoiding towns and villages which might slow the advance. Meanwhile his artillery and infantry engaged the French and kept them so busy that, by late afternoon, they were running out of fuel. When, at about 5.30 p.m., they were ordered to fall back only seven Chars B of the 28th could move and the 26th Tanks could muster only 20 of their Hotchkiss.

The 37th Tank Battalion had been in the thick of the battle. Fearing that 5th Panzer would outflank their comrades to the south, seven tanks of 2nd Company attacked with good effect but, by 2 p.m., the three remaining were in such bad state that their crews were obliged to destroy them themselves. At 4 p.m. the 1st and 3rd Companies, which had been lightly engaged, were ordered to fall back north-west towards Mettet. Fearing problems with crossing the River Molignée at Ermeton, 3rd Company made for Denée to the north-east, there to encounter the German VIII Corps, and be destroyed by their artillery. By the end of the day the 1st Armoured had only 20 fully operational tanks left. Of the 500 or so German tanks they had faced, about 10 per cent had been knocked out. Rommel said of the day:

'After a brief engagement with enemy tanks near Flavion, the Panzer Regiment advanced in column through the woods to Philippeville, passing on the way numerous guns and vehicles belonging to a French unit, whose men had tumbled headlong into the woods at the approach of our tanks … '

They exchanged fire with the French some three miles north-west of Philippeville and Rommel then turned south to prevent the French getting away in that direction. Rushing around in a great anti-clockwise sweep, the Germans gathered up hundreds of prisoners with little resistance. The shock of their presence was enough. By the evening Rommel was

some seven miles (11km) south-west of Philippeville, on the hills west of Cerfontaine.

'Looking back east from the summit of the hill, as night fell, endless pillars of dust could be seen rising as far as the eye could reach – comforting signs that the 7th Panzer Division's move into the conquered territory had begun.'

General Corap's new line of defence had been breached within 24 hours of its conception. Rommel was on the Frenchman's doorstep.

Further south the order to withdraw to a line through Rocroi had left the stubborn defenders of the Meuse at Monthermé in the lurch. The French 102nd Division was a fortress unit. The colonial machine-gunners, men from Indo-China and Madagascar, had no transport. In the early morning of 15 May, their flanks unsupported, they had been surrounded and overcome. The rest of the Ninth Army was collapsing behind them, whole units surrendering without firing a shot.

General Billotte telephoned General Georges to report the state of the 9th Army and to propose that General Henri Giraud, commander of the 7th Army, should take over. The change was effected at 4 a.m. on 16 May and Corap departed, in his own words, heartbroken.

Rommel was on the move once more on the morning of Thursday 16 May, pushing on over the French border at Clairfayts, ten miles (17km) south-east of Maubeuge. Here the extension of the Maginot line took the form of pillboxes with an anti-tank ditch, barbed wire and metal anti-tank obstacles called

ABOVE **A hastily taken photograph from the Rommel Collection bearing at least a resemblance to the location of the defences west of Clairfayts where Rommel fought his way through the extension of the Maginot Line.** (IWM RML 56)

RIGHT **An anti-tank ditch, barbed wire and hedgehogs supplemented the pillboxes along the Franco-Belgian border.** (IWM RML 100)

ABOVE **The advance west from the Canal des Ardennes. XIX Panzer Corps approach Omont, 15 May, 6 p.m.**

(B91/51/27A)

hedgehogs. The border was thus defended, but scarcely to the standard of the Maginot Line itself. Having been warned that the road through Clairfayts was mined, Rommel's column took to the fields and as they approached the village, he recounts,

'Suddenly we saw the angular outlines of a French fortification about 100 yards [90m] ahead. Close beside it were a number of fully-armed French troops who, at the first sight of the tanks, at once made as if to surrender. We were just beginning to think that we would be able to take it without fighting, when one of our tanks opened fire on the enemy elsewhere, with the result that the enemy garrison promptly vanished into their concrete pill-box. In a few moments the leading tanks came under heavy anti-tank gunfire from the left and French machine-gun fire opened over the whole area.'

The Germans responded with artillery fire and smoke, while the French artillery also plastered the area. German engineers crawled up and thrust a charge through the firing slit in the pillbox while sappers of 37th Reconnaissance Regiment blew up hedgehogs. With the coming of darkness Rommel, far from withdrawing to wait for the new day, pushed forward with renewed vigour, ordering a thrust as far as possible towards Avesnes. The Panzers silenced a troublesome artillery battery west of Clairfayts and, in Rommel's words,

'The way to the west was now open. The moon was up and for the time being we could expect no real darkness. I had already given orders … for the leading tanks to scatter the road and verges with machine and anti-tank gunfire at intervals during the drive to Avesnes … The mass of the division had instructions to follow up the Panzer Regiment lorry-borne.'

They rushed forward through the moonlight, now on the main road to Avesnes, clattering and roaring along. A burst of fire from a secondary defence line was answered with a fresh burst of fire and speed. Startled civilians and exhausted troops could only jerk from sleep to wonder at their passage.

'We drove through the villages of Sars Poteries and Beugnies with guns blazing. Enemy confusion was complete. Military vehicles, tanks, artillery and refugee carts packed high with belongings blocked part of the road and had to be pushed unceremoniously to the side. All around were French troops lying flat on the ground, and farms everywhere were jammed tight with guns, tanks and other military vehicles. Progress towards Avesnes became slow.'

Still in the dark they pushed on to curl west of

Avesnes on the Landrecies road where they paused at last. They had become separated from their support, but Rommel was not particularly concerned. It was clear there were plenty of French about, including part of the French 1st Armoured, 25th Battalion, with Hotchkiss H39s in the town itself. The 2/25th Panzer attacked but was unsuccessful, losing several tanks. At 4 a.m. on 17 May the Panzer IVs finally managed to overcome the French, effectively ending the existence of the French 1st Armoured Division.

Still Rommel gave his men no rest. The danger in Avesnes having been neutralised, they drove on for Landrecies where, shouting for the French traffic to make way, they made for the bridge over the River Sambre which they found intact. At 5.15 a.m. on Friday they stopped just east of Le Câteau. They had advanced more than 30 miles (50km) in 24 hours.

MONTCORNET AND CRÉCY

Early on Thursday 16 May, General Guderian drove through Vendresse and Omont to Bouvellemont, where he found Lieutenant-colonel Balck, red-eyed and dirty, had pushed his exhausted men on to take the village. They had followed Balck forward when, refusing to argue with officers who wanted to stop, he declared he would go on alone. Guderian now explained that, as a captured French order revealed, the French were in a state of near-panic and it was vital to maintain the pressure.

Guderian drove on, to Novion-Porcien and then on to Montcornet, about 30 miles (50km) from Bouvellemont. Here he found Generalmajor Werner Kempff of 6th Panzer in Reinhardt's Corps. There were now three Panzer divisions in the area and they agreed operational boundaries amongst themselves.

LEFT **The bridges at Moÿ de l'Aisne, over the river and the canal. This position, like others along the valley, was defended by a single tank.** (MME WW2/8/24)

BELOW **The memorial to the defenders of the Moÿ bridges.** (MME WW2/8/3)

Guderian gave the order to press on until fuel was exhausted, and by the end of the day German units had reached Marle and Dercy, another 25 miles (40km) to the west. That night Guderian settled in to rest at Soize, east of Montcornet, and made plans to continue the advance the next morning. Friday 17 May, brought a nasty surprise. An order arrived from Panzer Group to stay where he was and await a visit from General von Kleist. They met at the airstrip at 7 a.m. and Kleist delivered a tirade of condemnation for Guderian's excessive zeal.

The German High Command had always been worried about thrusting too far forward and exposing a vulnerable flank, but so far nothing had happened to reinforce their apprehension and Halder seemed to have joined the Manstein camp wholeheartedly. Hitler, however, was increasingly concerned about the southern flank and went to see Rundstedt, whose Army Group A War Diary reveals the view that

'The extended flank between La Fère and Rethel is too sensitive, especially in the Laon area … an open invitation for an enemy attack …'

Kleist also had been nervous throughout, and in this atmosphere his apprehensions had gained the upper hand. Guderian responded by offering his resignation. Kleist hesitated, startled, then nodded and told Guderian to hand over to the most senior of his subordinates, General Veiel. Guderian then signalled to Rundstedt his intention of going to Army Group headquarters, but was told to stay where he was and await Colonel-general List commander of the 12th Army.

List conveyed the order to Guderian that he was not to resign and produced a masterly compromise. Guderian's Corps headquarters was to stay put

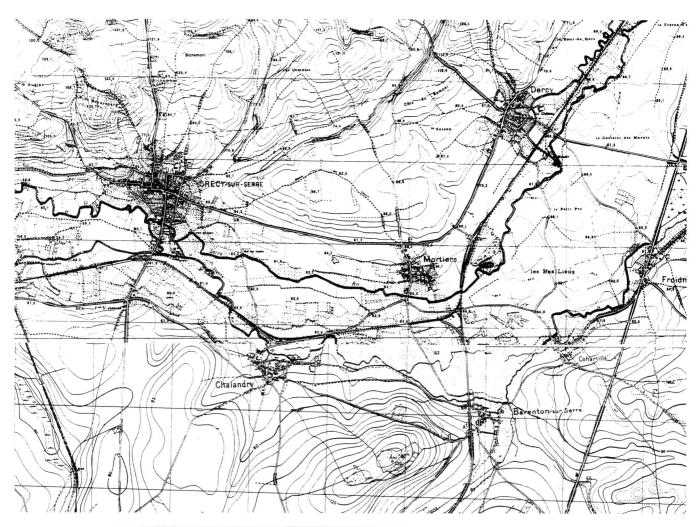

while the Panzers were authorised to carry out a reconnaissance in force. Guderian wrote:

'Then I set the "reconnaissance in force" in motion. Corps headquarters remained at its old location in Soize; a wire was laid from there to my advanced headquarters, so that I need not communicate with my staff by wireless and my orders could therefore not be monitored by the wireless intercept units of the OKH and the OKW'

Without the knowledge of Kleist or Rundstedt the advance would proceed.

The anticipated flank attack did take place. On 15 May Colonel Charles de Gaulle had been summoned to see General Georges. The new commander of the 4th Armoured Division was to receive his orders to delay the German advance while a new defence line was set up. Georges himself remarked:

'There, de Gaulle! For you who have so long held the ideas which the enemy is putting into practice, here is the chance to act.'

That such a remark could be made at this time is indicative of how little grasp Georges had of the true situation. Not only had the Panzers advanced too far to permit the establishment of the intended line, but the 4th Armoured Division was virtually non-existent.

OPPOSITE TOP **The scene of De Gaulle's second attack on Guderian's flank at Crécy-sur-Serre.** (BL C21 (15), sheets XXVII-9/5-6 and 10/1-2)

OPPOSITE BOTTOM **The village of Dercy from the south-east. The broad valley continues to Crécy, to the left, with the hills beyond.** (MME WW2/7/34)

LEFT **Signs of the French retreat at Péronne, photographed on 19 May.** (B91/46/5)

The 345th Tank Company (Renault D2s) reached Soissons on the way to the rendezvous near Laon on the morning of 16 May and 24th (Renault 35s) and 46th (Chars B) Tank Battalions arrived in the evening together with one company from the 2nd Battalion. The rest of his division, two tank battalions, four tank companies, the artillery and the regiments of infantry and cavalry, did not turn up. De Gaulle had to use what was to hand.

'I threw them forward as soon as daylight appeared. Sweeping away on their path the enemy units which were already invading that piece of country, they reached Montcornet. Till evening they fought on the outskirts of the place and within it ...'

The Renault 35s of 1/24th Tank Battalion entered Montcornet at noon, but immediately lost four tanks. The Renault B1bis of the 46th, having destroyed a German motorised column near Chivres-en-Laonnois, advanced between Clermont-les-Fermes, south-west, and Dizy-le-Gros, south of Montcornet. They were pushing on to the north, when their commander, Jean Bescond, was forced to abandon his broken-down vehicle and take over *Sampiero-Corso* to continue his attack. All its occupants died when, shortly thereafter, it was hit and exploded. The 4th Chasseurs joined de Gaulle that afternoon and were immediately sent into action against a German force that popped up at Chivres, behind the French advance. But the 4th Armoured lacked air, artillery or infantry support. De Gaulle wrote:

'... *From the north of the Serre the German artillery was firing on us. Our own was far from being in position. All the afternoon the Stukas, swooping out of the sky and returning ceaselessly, attacked our tanks and lorries. We had nothing with which to reply. Finally, German mechanised detachments, more and more numerous and active, began skirmishing in our rear. We were lost children thirty kilometres in advance of the Aisne, we had got to put an end to a situation that was, to say the least, risky.'*

The French withdrew with losses of 12 Chars B, 20 Renault 35s and some of the D2s, but it had inflicted loss on the Germans. Guderian, presumably distracted by his skirmish with his superiors, makes little mention of the fight, and apparently did not report it, perhaps lest it add fuel to the uneasiness of the German High Command.

That evening the Panzers had reached the river and canal barriers of the Oise and the Sambre to Oise Canal in their broad valley overlooked by gentle hills. The defence consisted of scattered armoured units, many positioned one tank per bridge in place of artillery and, what is more, without support of any kind. No matter how heroic their men, these isolated machines could not stand and they were plucked one by one. At 9 a.m. on Saturday 18 May 2nd Panzer had reached St Quentin.

De Gaulle's 4th Armoured had, by Saturday evening, been refreshed by the addition of various companies of armoured units to the tune of having 155 tanks. At 4 a.m. on Sunday 19 May they attacked once more, this time heading north of Laon towards Crécy-sur-Serre. The Renuault 35s of 2nd Tank

Battalion actually entered Crécy, but could go no further; the Germans defended the river and had the advantage of the heights beyond. By the end of the day, when the 4th Armoured withdrew once more, it had lost 10 Chars B, 20 Somua S-35s and close on 50 Renault 35s as well as a dozen armoured cars; half its strength. The Germans regarded the intervention as pretty trivial.

ON TO THE SEA

In early 1939 the 21-year-old Doug Swift, a gardener, got a job with Eastbourne Corporation. Within a year his employment was to be interrupted and Eastbourne was almost empty, the inhabitants evacuated as it was a town in the front line. He was called up in January 1940 and found himself in the 7th Battalion, the Royal Sussex Regiment. By April he was in France, in Argeuil, near Forges-les-Eaux, whence they were ordered to Lens to join the BEF in the defence of the Escaut. The train went by way of Amiens, he recalls.

'We came steaming slowly into St Roche station, Amiens, this was the morning of 18th May ... a Saturday. I was dozing on the floor of the truck with the

LEFT **A touching memorial in the communal cemetery in Péronne. The tombs of his countrymen who fell in the Franco-Prussian War are close by, as are those of British soldiers of 1914–18.**
(MME WW2/8/13)

BELOW **A Panzer unit, tanks and infantry, advancing across a Somme cornfield.**
(B73/2/12)

other chaps, it was a warm, dry day. The next thing we knew, this screaming noise was coming down at us. Then the bombs were falling, exploding amongst the trucks sending showers of debris flying high into the air, falling to the ground a few seconds later… We scrambled out of the trucks, diving underneath them just before the Stukas came screaming down for a second attack, followed by a third.'

The railway lines were torn up and dead and wounded lay everywhere. Swift's CO was wounded, so Lieutenant Jackson took over.

'I remember Lieutenant Jackson saying, about all the carnage and destruction, "It's a bad business, but that's war." And as this was our first taste of it, I thought "Well, I'm not looking forward to this very much."'

The Sussex moved away from the station to a nearby wood.

On Sunday 19 May 1st Panzer reached Péronne and forced a bridgehead over the canal, the last water obstacle before the Channel. The protection of the left flank was secured by bringing up 10th Panzer and 1st Panzer pushed on over the familiar ground of the First World War battlefield of the Somme, heading for Amiens. The 7th Royal West Kents were at Albert where 2nd Panzer were going. On the morning of Monday 20 May, Guderian set out in good time to see what would happen at Amiens, driving round Albert because it was still held by the British.

LEFT **The memorial to the 7th Sussex on the north-western side of the N29 between Amiens and Salouël.**
(MME WW2/9/36)

BELOW **The foundations of the château are marked in a clearing in the woods west of the Sussex memorial.**
(MME WW2/10/1)

ABOVE **Doug Swift's sketch of the battle of Monday 20 May. He says that C and D Companies may have been the other way round. The road in the foreground is the N29 from Amiens to Poix and the road in the distance is the N1 to Dury.**

OPPOSITE TOP **Refuelling at the expense of the French; Amiens, 11.45 a.m., 20 May.** (B71/86/68)

OPPOSITE BOTTOM **The morning after. Dead of the 7th Sussex photographed at 9 a.m., 21 May.** (B89/122/12A)

On Sunday the 7th Royal Sussex had moved out of town and up the hill to the south-west where a wood surrounded a château on the Amiens to Poix road. It was a busy road. Swift reports:

'Refugees were going by endlessly. All those that had cars had put mattresses on their tops as a bit of protection against machine gunning from the air. There were cars, lorries and horses and carts loaded with belongings, hand carts, bicycles, wheel barrows, anything that would carry a few possessions. People walking carrying suitcases, bundles in hands and on heads, streamed down the road past us away from the advancing German army.

'Amiens was a garrison town and out of it came pouring lorry-loads of French troops – the garrison was shoving off! I thought "This is a bit odd, the French garrison pushing off while we from another country wait for whatever was out there somewhere!"'

There the Sussex stayed all day, deployed in the field and in the wood, watching the German bombers pound Amiens into ruins. The next morning they were still there, the French Commandant of the town having no orders for them. Doug Swift and his comrades asked why the big shells were whizzing over

their heads. French artillery practising, they were told. Then some figures appeared in the valley to their east. Jerries, someone said. An old man was pushing his handcart across the field. A lone French soldier came along with his rifle and lay down beside them. Sharing no language they nodded and smiled. A French light tank was persuaded to stay with them. They waited. Swift takes up the tale:

'I never did fill in the will form in the back of my Pay Book. Seemed too final, somehow … The weather was quiet, warm, sunny and dry… Without any warning, a hail of machine gun bullets came sweeping down amongst us from German tanks on the top road. We commenced firing back, the light French tank opened up and immediately became a target for heavy mortars. They came whistling over … finally knocking it out. They were also hitting the château with heavy mortars, causing considerable damage and the farm buildings on our right front were on fire… I noticed that the speeds and the sounds of the bullets varied, some went by with a terrific zip, others whined by. Some were high pitched and urgent … while others droned by and one or two seemed spent.'

The Sussex were utterly out-gunned. A lorry attempting to bring up ammunition was hit and exploded. The battle continued through the afternoon. At about 5 p.m. the Battalion Headquarters in the château was overrun but the men out in the field fought on until the tanks poured down from the road. Those who could stand rose slowly to surrender.

'The old man who had been trundling his little handcart was lying in a heap, dead, his cart on its side. The little lone French soldier lay stretched out dead beside his rifle. He was the hero of France, giving his life for his country while his compatriots had scurried off.'

Swift found that the front-line troops treated them with respect. The wounded survivors were gathered up and taken to hospital. The unwounded, some 70 men from the 700 or so that had arrived on the train only a couple of days before, marched into captivity. As they went the Germans they encountered became less charming, food and water meagre. They reached Bastogne before, half starving, they were put onto a train for Poland and prison camp.

Guderian was well pleased with the morning's events. He regarded the action at Amiens, intended to secure a bridgehead rather than a break-through, as complete by noon and turned back for Albert. There the West Kents had fought as hard as the Sussex. Swift saw the results as he marched through. Lorries burnt out and dead, burned men strewn around. Guderian found 2nd Panzer, claiming insufficient fuel, halted. They were quickly on the move again, for Abbeville, which they reached by 5 p.m. During the night the

ABOVE **Rommel's coloumn passes an abandoned French Somua S-35.** (IWM RML 70)

RIGHT **A pillbox near the Roman road running north-east of Bavay, between Valenciennes and Maubeuge. This is much fought-over country; a few miles beyond is Malplaquet, scene of Marlborough's bloody and hollow victory of 1709.** (MME WW2/4/20)

Spitta Battalion of 2nd Panzer reached the sea near Noyelles. The Allies were cut in two. The next day there were no orders about which way they should go next, so Guderian

'… spent the day visiting Abbeville and our crossings and bridgeheads over the Somme. On the way I asked the men how they had enjoyed the operations up to date. "Not bad," said an Austrian of the 2nd Panzer Division, "but we wasted two whole days." Unfortunately, he was right.'

RETURN TO CAMBRAI

General Rommel was in a precarious position on the morning of Friday 17 May, but, luckily for him, the French did not know it. Their 2nd Armoured Division had been cut in two by Guderian's galloping progress, with part of it south of the Aisne and involved in General de Lattre de Tassigny's stubborn defence of Rethel, while the rest had been scattered across the front in an attempt to bar the Oise crossings. Rommel himself was annoyed that the rest of his division had failed to match his cracking pace and turned back to gather them up. With a Panzer III accompanying his signals vehicle, off he went, back the way he had come, through Landrecies, where they got lost, past a burnt-out German tank on the Avesnes road and onwards. The escorting tank fell out with mechanical trouble, so on went Rommel in his lone, unarmoured vehicle.

East of Marolles they came upon a Panzer IV. Rommel was relieved! One or two other German units were turning up and, comforted that he was not entirely alone, Rommel pushed on. French troops were encountered and ordered to have their vehicles fall in behind the signals vehicle. By the time he got to Avesnes, Rommel was being followed by about 40 French trucks which were then marshalled in a field so that their occupants could be disarmed. By 4 p.m.

ABOVE **The forts around Maubeuge resisted but were ill-equipped and eventually fell. Fort de Leveau is being restored and preserved.** (MME WW2/4/22)

LEFT **Memorial to the 87th Regiment and to an individual, Ernest Delalain, at Fort de Leveau.** (MME WW2/4/23)

Rommel's staff had caught up with him and the area overrun was in the process of being consolidated.

On Saturday 18 May the objective was Cambrai, scene of the great tank battle of the First World War. However, the 25th Panzer Regiment in front of Le Câteau was low on fuel and ammunition and had to be resupplied. Moreover, elements of the French 2nd Armoured Division with Renault B1s had inserted themselves between Rommel and the forward unit. He wrote:

'I later caught up with the Panzer Battalion in the wood half a mile east of Pommereuille, and found them in violent action against French tanks which were barring the road. Violent fighting developed on the road and there was no chance of outflanking the enemy position on either side. Our guns seemed to be completely ineffective against the heavy armour of the French tanks.'

Rommel decided to leave them to it and get on to the 25th, by way of Ors to the south where there was a bridge. The supply column failed to follow, so all he could do was try to cheer up the commander of the stymied Panzer regiment and call up enough force to free the road through Pommereuille. By 3 p.m. this was done and the advance towards Cambrai became possible.

'I now gave orders for the reinforced Battalion Paris [the name of the commander] to secure the roads leading from Cambrai to the north-east and north as quickly as possible. Led by its few tanks and two troops of self-propelled AA guns, the battalion advanced over a broad front and in great depth straight across the fields to the north-west, throwing up a great cloud of dust as they went.'

So impressive was the demonstration that no one guessed these were mostly thin-skinned vehicles. They scattered fire into the northern outskirts of Cambrai as they went. No resistance was offered.

Most of the next day, Sunday, was devoted to rest and resupply. But for the evening a further advance was planned. General Hoth, the Corps commander, thought this was asking too much of the men, but Rommel persuaded him otherwise. Early in the morning of Monday, 20 May, they were off again, but without the same luck. The over-extended line of advance was penetrated by the French and it took some time to bring up an infantry regiment to secure the line of communication. To the north the German armour formerly engaged in the Gembloux gap had pushed southward to take the forts around Maubeuge. Here, on Rommel's front, it was decided to consolidate south of Arras, for the news had come that the Allies were pulling out of Belgium and the opposition before them was hardening. It would have to, for the Allies in the north were now in the embrace of a German presence from the mouth of the Somme to the Belgian coast.

BELOW **French troops surrender in the Bois de l'Evéque.** (IWM RML 63)

RETURN TO FLANDERS FIELDS

Lord Gort was not a flamboyant soldier. His courage was undoubted. He had won the V.C. in September 1918 leading the Grenadier Guards to take Prémy Ridge near Graincourt, an action in which he was twice wounded. He was loyal and dutiful, and saw his task as to obey the orders received from his superior officer, General Billotte. He had one overriding order, to the effect that if he thought the security of the BEF was compromised, he had a right of appeal to London. Gort's staff got on well with the French staff. In these circumstances it was disturbing to him that Billotte communicated with him so little. It was even more disturbing when, a week after the German attack, he did.

On the night of 18-19 May Billotte went to Gort's headquarters at Wahagnies. The orders, counter-orders and changes of plan of the previous few days were now summed up in Billotte's remark: 'Je suis crevé de fatigue, et contre ces Panzers je ne peux rien faire.' (I'm worn out and against these panzers I can do nothing.) Churchill's flying visit to Paris on 16 May had discovered no coherent fighting policy either, but he still did everything possible to keep their spirits up, including persuading the British Cabinet to agree to more fighter squadrons being sent to France. It was becoming increasingly clear that, unless something

remarkable took place to prevent it, the French High Command was cracking up. Gort had, on 17 May, in order to secure the BEF against the collapse of their southern flank, created a special task force, Macforce, under Major-general Mason-Macfarlane, his Director of Military Intelligence. Quite why this was the time to dispense with the services of the Director of Military Intelligence is unclear. Now, on 19 May, in spite of the fact that General Georges had just removed Arras from the BEF's zone, Gort established Petreforce under General R. L. Petrie to defend the town. Further, the Englishman's thoughts were turning to what might be done if the French effort to close the great gap through which the Germans were pouring should fail. That he was examining the possibility of a withdrawal on Dunkirk became known to London at 4.30 p.m. that Sunday and, because the Cabinet favoured falling back on the lines of communication south of the Somme, Field Marshal Lord Ironside was sent out to put Gort right.

In Paris the return of General Weygand was awaited. He had been summoned from Syria by Prime Minister Reynaud. Meanwhile General Gamelin was taking a personal interest in events. On Sunday he went to General Georges's headquarters where he drafted 'Personal and Secret Instruction No. 12', which began:

LEFT **A German bicycle squadron. A barge forms part of a bridge for crossing the Maas-Scheldt Canal in northern Belgium.** (B78/126/4A)

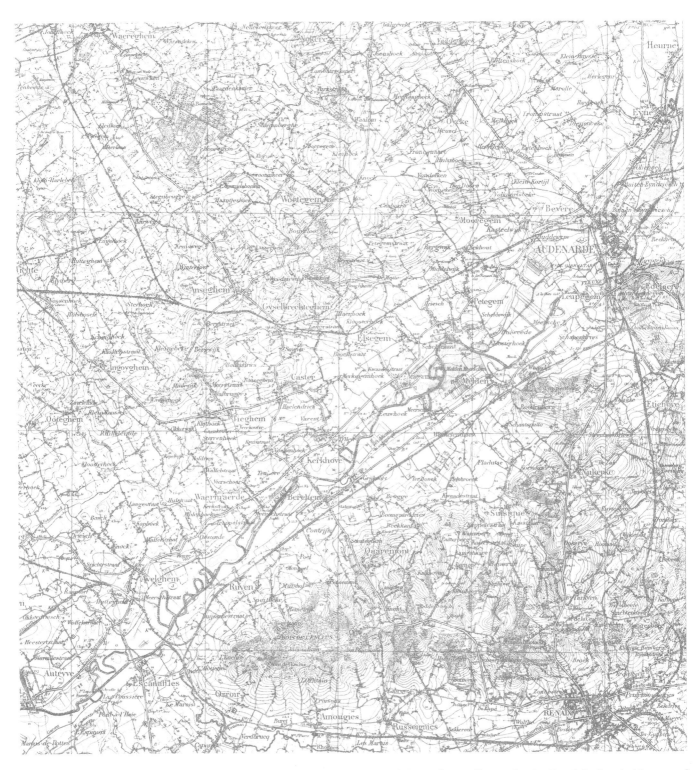

'Without wishing to interfere in the conduct of the battle now being waged, which is in the hands of the Commander-in-Chief of the North-East Front …'

and went on to suggest, rather vaguely, that the advanced Panzer divisions should be stopped on the Somme and also attacked in their rear where there appeared to be, he said, a vacuum at that time. In addition there should be an attack on Mézières and an all-out effort in the air. Certainly the pinching out of the salient created by the Panzers was a sound, not to say a classic, plan, but it was all too languid and all too late. At 3.30 p.m. Weygand called on Gamelin and asked to be brought up to date on events, then for permission to call on Georges. Just five hours later Gamelin received a letter from Weygand informing him that the writer was replacing him.

OPPOSITE LEFT **Belgian military map of the Escaut line south of Audenarde (Oudenarde), the area in which Major Lord Sysonby and the 1/5th Queens fought close to the railway line running west. The American 91st Division liberated Audenarde in 1918 and Marlborough fought north of the town in 1708.** (MME WW2Maps MF2/17)

LEFT **The market square at Ypres with the Cloth Hall on the left and the cathedral spire on the right.** (MME Ypres 5/4)

BELOW **A Panzer IV passing a British Bren Carrier, possibly in Ficheux, south-west of Arras, on 21 May.** (IWM RML 139)

The 73-year-old Weygand had had a terrible journey and, after two days on the move to Paris and around France, was exhausted. Monday 20 May was therefore devoted to resting, though not before Gamelin's order No.12 of the previous day had been cancelled. This was the day that Guderian's men reached the Channel.

ON THE ESCAUT

Major Lord Sysonby was probably feeling a little fatigued as well, but the cause was different. Sunday, 19 May, had been spent in attempting to control the tide of civilians and soldiers pouring west over the Escaut. Early in the day he had been able to write home, telling the sad story of the barge people being turned off their boats on the Escaut so the engineers could sink them. He did not get the time to write again until Thursday. The 1/5th Queens Royal Regiment were next to the railway south-west of Audenarde near Petegem, and forward of them were 1/6th Queens, overlooking the river and the lowland around Melden on the south-eastern bank. At noon on Monday enemy cyclists were seen coming down the hill into Melden and in the afternoon the Germans attempted to reach the river, but were shot down. A more cautious approach led to numerous German penetrations on a small scale and the day passed in a succession of counter-attacks. Meanwhile, to the south near Valenciennes, the French closed the sluices in an attempt to flood their front. As a result, here the water level was going down, draining the ditches in the marshy water-meadows and providing cover for attackers. During the night Petegem village fell to the Germans. Sysonby was summoned and told:

'The situation is critical as they will get round behind us… Take the Carrier platoon and go in there and restore the situation… We advanced towards this village [Petegem] some seven miles away at high speed and on reaching it were truly appalled at the spectacle. Most of the houses were on fire, large explosions were going on all over the town caused by the extremely heavy barrage of German shells fired from heavy guns. The air was so filled with smoke from the burning houses and the cordite fumes that is was hard to see… We advanced down the main street which was nothing more than a shambles of dead men and animals intermingled with great piles of rubble. I noticed a very gallant action of machine-gunners giving overhead fire in an easterly direction all unperturbed by the inferno raging around them.'

Turning left at the cross-roads, Sysonby saw a column of Germans marching three abreast. Many died under the Queen's fire. One 'singly brave' German fired his anti-tank rifle at Sysonby, narrowly missing, and then went to throw a grenade.

'I shot him in the face with my revolver which was a very fluky shot as we were travelling at about 20mph

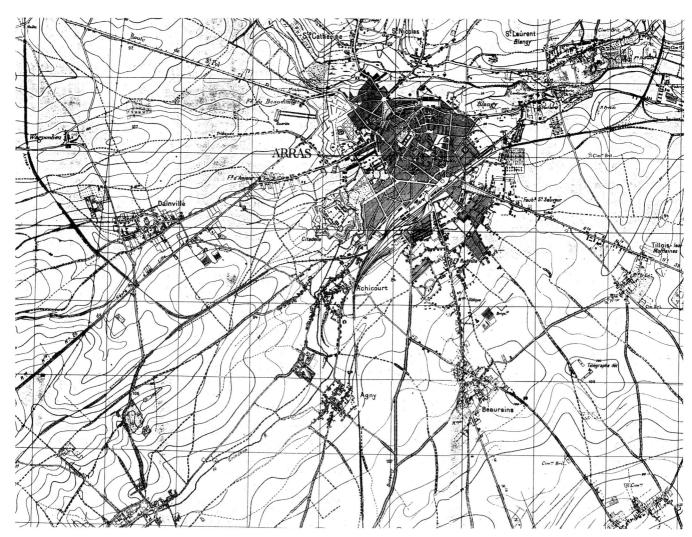

ABOVE **Arras: (pages 88-91)** a
composite of German
1:25,000 maps made after the
occupation. Road
improvements and new
buildings have obscured
some of the ground,
particularly south-east and
east of Arras and the N25 to
the south-west has been
upgraded. The ridge north-
west of Wailly (village bottom
left) is little altered except for
the abandonment of the light
railway, the bed of which
remains. Given the excellence
of the sight-lines, it is
remarkable that Rommel
exaggerated the British
strength so greatly.

(BL C21 (15) sheets XXIV-6/5-6 and 7-8)

*[30kph]. We then proceeded on our course for about a
mile and a half [2.5km] into the enemy's lines shooting all
and sundry we saw.'*

They turned and started back to the village, now
taking the Germans in the rear. A carrier had been hit
and immobilised, its driver, Corporal Peters, stuck in
it with a smashed thigh and trapped foot, and two
of its crew made prisoner. Sysonby's return journey
scared off their captors and gave Sergeant Wynn the
chance to rescue Peters, a deed for which he received
the DCM.

That afternoon the Germans shelled Petegem into
dust and the Queens were forced to fall back. Sysonby
was ordered to remain with the 5th Royal Sussex at
Huttegem, east of Vichte, six miles (10km) west of
Petegem. He wrote:

*'We got about two hours sleep and then took up our
positions on a ridge facing the enemy. We had only one
spade between us, the others having been smashed in the
action the day before, so we had to dig little holes for
ourselves ...'*

As they dug the shelling started but did little more
than scare them stiff. Stragglers were coming in and

Sysonby reformed the men into 'Z' Company, a
makeshift unit of which its members appeared
curiously proud. In the afternoon the shelling began
again in good earnest and all they could do was huddle
down in their trenches. Sysonby reported to the
Colonel commanding the Sussex and as they talked a
shell entered the dug-out.

*'The man standing next to me had his head cut clean
off but neither the Colonel or I were touched although
considerably shaken. My orders were to take the carrier
platoon up on the ridge and to try and save the situation
by frightening the Germans as they are reputed to be
afraid of armoured fighting vehicles. I had a look round
the position which was hard to see owing to the incessant
flashes and clouds of cordite smoke but quickly realised
were I to obey this order the carrier platoon would be
wiped out to a man.'*

Instead they made a brief demonstration and fell
back before the Germans could respond. Passing
through the burning village they were asked to stay
and stiffen the Sussex's line, which they did.

*'We fixed bayonets and got ready. The Germans came
on steadily and we gave them as good as they gave us. The*

most unattractive part of the programme was their firing at us with sub machine-guns with tracer bullets.'

Sysonby stayed on with eight men to cover the retreat and the Germans responded with a heavy box barrage which set light to the surrounding woods.

'You can imagine how near to hell it was with burning woods, the reek of cordite and its pungent brown smoke mixing with the smoke of burning trees. The incessant flashes and roaring reports from the shells and the tracer ammunition stabbing the twilight like furious fireflies. By luck we managed to slip down a sunken bank and I took a swift compass bearing on a distant church … on the line of retreat.'

They set off cross-country, avoiding the shell-deluged roads, and five hours later Sysonby brought his men out on a safe road and marched them through the night to rejoin the battalion. He was awarded the DSO for his actions in these three days.

The French were offering battle as well. The evidence of their determination was found by the Earl of Cardigan after the storm had passed, but not before he had also found defensive positions that seemed untouched. Cardigan had been captured but had escaped and was making his way south from Belgium in an attempt, successful eventually, to reach southern France and return home to England. He went cautiously up along the banks of the river Escault and had reached a point just to the north of Valenciennes. He wrote in 1940:

'The detour to avoid the Kommandantur at Condé was not as easy as it might have been, for here were some of the former French defences – great stretches of barbed wire still forming an impassable barrier to a man on foot. Oddly enough the French do not seem to have attempted to hold this carefully prepared ground – for I could detect few signs of fighting – but maybe the position was turned and had to be abandoned to avoid encirclement.'

Having circumnavigated Condé, Cardigan re-gained the river and examined the terrain. The waterway was canalised and here was above the level of the surrounding country. There was no evidence of the western side being reinforced, with a parapet for example, or of the natural cover to the east being cleared away. The presence of graves showed that there had been fighting and Cardigan could imagine small groups of Germans working forward through the bushes before springing a surprise attack.

'To me the scattered French graves, encountered everywhere in groups of three or four or half a dozen, seem particularly tragic: here lie men who, making a stand in their own little sector, sacrificed everything to defend their country, while perhaps only a few miles away great gaps had been torn in the line of defence, allowing the tide of the German invasion to flow in behind and around them. They at least, whether aware of the threatening disaster or ignorant of it, held their ground to the last.'

THE CRUMBLING ALLIANCE

Lord Ironside reached Gort's headquarters early on Monday 20 May. He still thought that the Panzers to the south were present in penny packets and could be mopped up by the BEF He was soon fully appraised of the situation. From the north Bock's Army Group B was pressing back the Belgians and the British while Rommel threatened Arras and Guderian Abbeville. Gamelin's last order had already been countermanded, but all Gort could offer, he explained, was a strike around Arras co-ordinated with an attack by General René Altmayer's V Corps towards Cambrai. The isolation of the Panzers had to depend on an attack from the Somme. Ironside accepted this and next visited Billotte in an attempt to spur the French commander into positive action.

Weygand was now rested and taking control. He issued an order to keep civilians off the roads except between 6 p.m. and midnight, thus giving some freedom of movement to his troops. He also

ABOVE **Two British graves in Wailly communal cemetery.**
(MME WW2/4/12)

LEFT **French tanks also fought Rommel's force on 21 May.**
(MME WW2/4/11)

discovered that the only way to speak to Billotte was through an unreliable telephone link via London. He decided to go visiting. London was informed and sent Gort a message to say Weygand was coming the next day. Unfortunately the message, dictated on Monday 20 May, was not dispatched until early the next morning. It therefore bore the date of 21 May and still said 'tomorrow'.

At 9 a.m. on Tuesday 21 May, Weygand took off from Le Bourget and flew north, over the battlefield of the Somme where the Panzers' progress was clear to see, and landed at Norrent-Fontes, midway between St Omer and Béthune. Apparently there was no one there. A man with an old truck was found who gave them a lift into the village to make a telephone call at the post office. Contact once made with 1st Army Group Headquarters, they flew on to St-Inglevert, south-west of Calais, and Weygand met General Pierre Champon, head of the French Military Mission at the Belgian headquarters. Together they drove off for Ypres. The inter-Allied conference consisted of King Leopold and General van Overstraeten for the Belgians, the two recently arrived Frenchmen and Admiral Sir Roger Keyes, the British representative to King Leopold, to be joined later that afternoon by Generals Billotte and Falgade. But no Gort. Weygand's plan for an attack from both north and south demanded a retreat by the Belgians to protect the British flank. The Belgians argued against it. Keyes was sent to look for Gort, but by the time he had located him and brought him back to Ypres, Weygand had left to take ship from Dunkirk for Cherbourg and return

to Paris. Nothing was settled. It is astounding that Weygand embarked on such a journey without adequate planning and equally astonishing that Gort should leave his headquarters without making sure he could be contacted. The day was wasted while the Germans progressed. The generals dispersed in the growing darkness. On the way to Douai Billotte's car crashed. The French general was fatally injured and died two days later. The co-ordination of the Allies was yet further compromised.

THE COUNTER-ATTACK AT ARRAS

At the last minute Altmayer's contribution to the attack to the south was cancelled. It is said that a messenger found him sitting on his bed, weeping. The British went ahead. Major-general Harold Franklyn headed another of the ad-hoc formations, Frankforce. The force was small. Instead of two divisions he had three infantry battalions, 6th, 7th and 8th Durham Light Infantry and two tank battalions, 4th and 7th Royal Tank Regiment. Only one of the Tank battalions, the 7th, had any of the more modern Mark IIs, the Matildas, of which there were 16, so out of those seven were attached to the 4th. There were 58 Mark Is altogether. These tanks were badly in need of servicing and renewals of parts, especially tracks. The trains that had been intended to bring them back from the Dyle line had failed through lack of drivers, so the AFVs had been driven to France with consequent wear and tear on their tracks. Two field artillery batteries, two anti-tank batteries and a motor-cycle battalion for reconnaissance completed the force. On their right the undaunted General Prioux of the French Cavalry Corps put his 3rd Light Mechanised Division, with about 70 tanks, into the field, worn though it was from the fighting in the Gembloux Gap.

The command of the operation was given to Major-general G. le Q. Martel, commander of 50th Division. The tanks were to advance in two columns west of Arras, the stated objective being to secure the town which Petreforce was preparing to defend. The intelligence was that some Panzers were present to the south of Arras, but their numbers were not believed to be great. Frankforce assembled, having made its way over roads crowded with refugees and straying soldiers, at Vimy. Maps were in short supply, most of the radios were out of action and there was no equipment for communication between the tanks and the infantry. Nor was liaison with their artillery any more organised. Of air support there was none. In this sorry state Frankforce went into battle, leaving Vimy at 11 a.m. on Tuesday 21 May and crossing their start line at 2 p.m.

With the 12th Lancers perched up on Mont St Eloi on the west, the right column (7th Royal Tank Regiment and 8th Durham Light Infantry) was to pass below the hill through Maroeuil, Warlus and Wailly, while the left column (4th RTR and 6th DLI) wrapped itself closer to Arras through Achicourt and Beaurins. True to form, Rommel had decided to respond to the resistance offered by the British in Arras by going round them, so 7th Panzer was coming round the south of Arras with the SS Division

Totenkopf on its left along the route intended for Martel's right column, while 5th Panzer was heading towards the east of the town on a collision course with the left column. Rommel had been chasing up laggard Rifle Regiments when he came under fire from a point to the north of Ficheux and Wailly. At the northern exit from Wailly he found one of his howitzer batteries firing on tanks approaching from the north. The British had already overcome Germans in Duisans and Warlus, but missed the 25th Panzer Regiment which was pushing north, and to the west the French had cleared Agnes and Simoncourt and were approaching the Arras-Doulens road. Rommel was confident his howitzers could hold their own and turned his attention to the situation in Wailly.

'The enemy [British and French] tank fire had created chaos and confusion among our troops in the village and they were jamming up the roads and yards with their vehicles, instead of going into action with every available weapon to fight off the oncoming enemy... We drove off to a hill 1,000 yards west of the village ... About 1,200 yards west of our position, the leading enemy tanks [of 7th RTR], among them one heavy, had already crossed the Arras-Beaumetz railway and shot up one of our Panzer IIIs. At the same time several enemy tanks were advancing down the road from Bac du Nord [on the Arras-Doullens road] and across the railway line to Wailly. It was an extremely tight spot ...'

What Rommel did not know was the 7th RTR had lost cohesion through radio failure and casualties

FAR LEFT **The 4th Dragons Portées are commemorated at St Eloi.** (MME Yp/Ar 7/30)

LEFT **Also at St Eloi, British graves. These are men of 208 Battery, 52nd Anti-Tank Regiment, Royal Artillery, who died on 22 May in the aftermath of the Arras attack.** (MME Yp/Ar 7/29)

ABOVE **A Matilda Mark II knocked out at Arras. A jubilant soldier points out the shell hole.** (B127/399/16A)

and were no longer acting in concert. What he did see was

'The crew of a howitzer battery, some distance away, now left their guns, swept along by the retreating infantry. With [Oberleutnant Joachim] Most's help, I brought every available gun into action at top speed against the tanks … I personally gave each gun its target… We ran from gun to gun… We now directed our fire against the other group of tanks attacking from the direction of Bac du Nord, and succeeded in keeping the tanks off, setting fire to some, halting others and forcing the rest to retreat… The worst seemed to be over and the attack beaten off, when suddenly Most sank to the ground …'

Martel's left column had made better progress, but eventually ran into heavy shellfire between Tilloy and Beaurins. Peter Vaux was with 4th Tanks that day and tells of the impact with the Germans on and around Telegraph Hill, between Beaurins and Tilloy.

'I could see … upwards of twenty tanks, down in the valley, just short of the potato clamp. The Colonel's tank was down there, a little in front of them – I could see it quite clearly, it was stationary and I could see the flag flying from it. The Adjutant's tank was quite close to the Colonel's, but from where I was I wasn't quite sure what to do, so I called up the Colonel … I called and I called and I called, but got no answer, and the Adjutant came on the air and he just said, "Come over and join me." So I motored down the valley … I saw that there were a

whole number of German anti-tank guns in the area of the potato clamp and crews were running about.'

Vaux also realised that field-gun fire was coming down from the wooded areas and from the crest line beyond. He drove on through the still tanks of his comrades,

'… I thought it very odd that they weren't moving and they weren't shooting, and I noticed that there was something even odder about them – because their guns were pointing at all angles; a lot of them had their turret hatches open and some of their crews were half in and half out of the tanks, lying wounded and dead – and I realised then, suddenly, with a shock, that all these twenty tanks had been knocked out, and that they had been knocked out by these big guns and they were, in fact, dead – all these tanks… At any rate, I went forward as I had been told to do, and joined the Adjutant among those German anti-tank guns.'

They began firing at the Germans and Vaux says he owed his life to the marksmanship of the Adjutant. The angle of Vaux's tank on the potato clamp, an earthen storage heap, prevented the gunner bringing his weapon to bear. Vaux was standing half out of the turret shouting instructions to gunner and driver while behind him a German was taking careful aim with his rifle on the back of the young man's head. The Adjutant shot the German with his revolver – another fluky shot! They silenced the anti-tank guns and sprayed the woods with machine-gun fire before retiring, field-gun shells falling all around them.

'As we drove back though the Matildas my heart sank because I realised what had happened: there were all those tanks I knew so well … there were the faces of those men with whom I had played games, swum, lived with for years – lying there dead … In that valley, the best of crews, our tanks, our soldiers, our officers were left behind.'

As darkness approached the Allies were scattered in little parcels about the field, as were the Germans. With night falling both sides withdrew towards their original positions. The British positions in Arras itself had been consolidated, but German attacks continued the next day, Wednesday 22 May, when 5th Panzer swept around the south-west and headed north while the German 12th Infantry Division was hurried up to attack on the river Scarpe north-east of Arras. They were stoutly opposed by 4th Green Howards and 2nd Wiltshire, but managed to cross the river. On 23 May at 7 p.m. the order was given to abandon Arras and defend the line of the Canal d'Aire through Béthune, some 15 miles (25km) to the north.

The use of the tanks was the subject of a note that Brigadier Vyvyan Pope, Gort's adviser on AFVs, wrote on 26 May and, lest he be killed or captured, gave to Brigadier D. H. Pratt, commander of 1st Army Tank Brigade to take back to the War Office. In it he said that there were essential facts learned as a result of bitter experience. First, there had to be a Commander, Royal Armoured Corps, in the field reporting to General Staff and in control of all armoured forces.

'We must model ourselves on German lines in this connection. You will be staggered to learn that 1st Army Tank Brigade marched and counter-marched the better part of 300 miles [480km] to fight one action. PRATT will tell you details. Similarly 3rd RTR has been thrown away.'

He went on to say that better armour and a bigger gun were needed.

'The 2-pdr. is good enough now, but only just. We must mount something better and put it behind 40 to 80mm of armour.'

The other points made were that 75% of casualties had been due to mechanical failure, road speeds were too slow, movement by rail was not to be relied on and that the Armoured Reconnaissance Brigade was a wash-out, unable to fight a delaying action but acceptable for reconnaissance alone. He concluded:

'I do hope the Powers that be realise that the Boche has succeeded solely because of his mass of tanks supported by air attack. Man for man we can beat him any day and twice a day, but dive-bombing followed by tank attack is too much on our very extended fronts. If only 1st Armoured Division had been out here in time, it might have made all the difference.'

The misuse of 1st Armoured by Weygand was yet to come.

Ironside had reported to Churchill on Sunday 19 May, and it was at last understood that only two courses were open to Gort, either to batter his way

LEFT **German losses at Arras. In the foreground a burnt out SdKfz 263 six-wheeled radio armoured car and, beyond, an SdKfz 231 eight-wheeled armoured car.** (IWM RML 125)

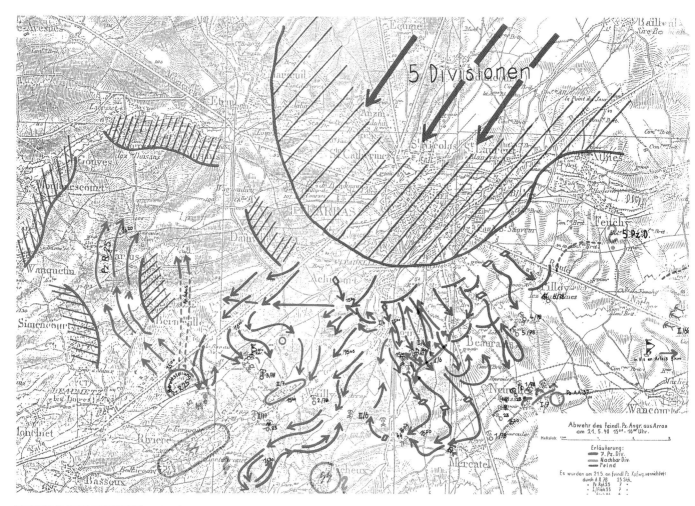

southwards, very unlikely to be successful, or prepare
to fall back to Dunkirk and attempt a sea evacuation.
Churchill was travelling again, and on that Wednesday
was in Paris. He was encouraged, doubtless eager to be
encouraged, by Weygand's obvious vigour and heartily
approved of his plan to cut off the head of the German
advance with combined attacks by General Frére's new
French 7th Army in the south and the eight divisions
assumed to be available from the Allies in the north. It
was a plan almost identical to Gamelin's which
Weygand had so precipitately cancelled when there
might yet have been time to make it work. It was a
plan now so far removed from reality that it is evident
that neither Weygand or his staff knew what was going
on. Nor did Churchill. He signalled to Gort the same
day, saying the Belgians were to fall back on the Yser
(which they had already declined to do), and that the
notional eight divisions would join hands with the
equally notional new army on the Somme in the
south. When Gort pulled his men back to the Canal
d'Aire on Thursday, the French declared that they had
been abandoned in what was becoming a salient east
of Lille by a British retreat 25-mile (40km) towards
the sea! The Weygand plan was thus impossible to
perform, though Gort was still preparing for it, in the

form of a sortie, on Friday. He repeated to Churchill
that the key lay in the attack from the south as he did
not have the ammunition to mount a grand offensive.
Perhaps, in Paris, they believed the false report of
British retreat, but in any case the bickering between
the Allies was increasing.

The great attack from the north was a plan that
died on Saturday 25 May. The Belgian line broke at
Courtrai, 15 miles (25km) north-east of Lille, the
Germans were over the River Lys and the British
acquired a major piece of intelligence that revealed
Bock's plan to hurl two corps of Army Group B
towards Ypres. The troops intended for the
southwards stroke, the 5th and 50th Divisions, were
immediately switched north to deal with the crisis.
Gort gave the order at 6.30 p.m. and General
Blanchard, Billotte's successor, had no option but
formally to cancel the Weygand scheme.

THE GERMAN UNCERTAINTY

All was not sweetness and light amongst the Germans
either. Rommel had excused his force's performance
against the British tanks by claiming that five divisions
had attacked. This confirmed German fears about
their vulnerable flanks. Guderian remarks:

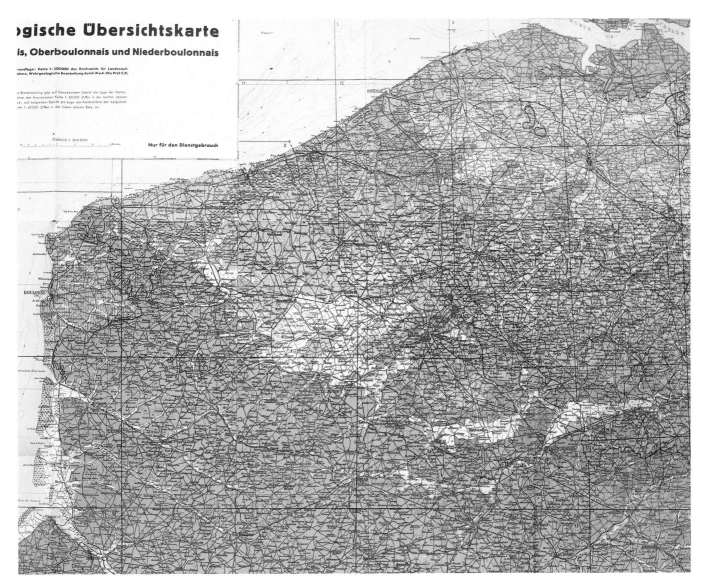

ABOVE **The German army
geological map, published in
Berlin 29 February 1940. The
description of terrain around
Dunkirk given in the text
(page 95) applies to the
purple area. The blue areas
inland of that are similar to
the terrain north-east of
Ypres in front of the ridge
crowned by Passchendaele. A
firm ridge runs from Guines,
just south of Calais, through
Ardres, branching south-east
towards St Omer and north-
east through Watten towards
Bergues. (MME WW2Maps MF2/5)**

'On 21st of May a noteworthy event occurred to the north of us: English tanks attempted to break through in the direction of Paris… The English did not succeed in breaking through, but they did make a considerable impression on the staff of Panzer Group von Kleist, which suddenly became remarkably nervous.'

On Wednesday 22 May Guderian was on the move again, to the north.

'In the afternoon … there was fierce fighting at Desvres, Samer and to the south of Boulogne. Our opponents were mostly Frenchmen, but included a number of English and Belgian units and even an occasional Dutchman. Their resistance was broken. But the enemy airforce was very active, bombing us and firing their guns at us too, while we saw little of our Luftwaffe. The bases from which our planes were operating were now a long way away …'

The British were also, from the other side of the Channel, flying within the outer area of their radar cover and out of secure airfields in England. In spite of their efforts Guderian's 2nd Panzer entered the outskirts of Boulogne that evening. Guderian now regained command of 10th Panzer and made fresh dispositions.

'I decided to move 1st Panzer Division, which was already close to Calais, on to Dunkirk at once, while the 10th Panzer Division, advancing from Doullens through Samer, replaced it in front of Calais. There was no particular urgency about capturing this port.'

The danger of Guderian getting up along the Channel coast behind Gort was now severe.

THE CANAL D'AIRE

On Monday 20 May the 1st Royal Irish Fusiliers, the Faughs as they called themselves, were ordered to hold a length of the Canal d'Aire at Béthune and eastwards through Gorre and Cuinchy to La Bassée, which was held by 7th Queens Royal Regiment. It was an immense length to allocate to a single battalion. They had been in tough action at Ninove, east of

Audenarde, the previous Saturday, but were now comforted by being back in a country for which they had decent 1-inch maps. Captain John Horsfall's D Company was at Gorre, where three bridges cross the canal; one lofted the road to Lens over the water by approach embankments, the second was a puny foot-bridge connecting the railway station on the south bank with the rest of the village, and there was a third bridge further east. On Tuesday he inspected the Lens-road bridge.

'There I found four sappers resident, sitting on ammunition boxes and busy frying their breakfast. Until our arrival these four were, I think, the only troops in occupation of our sector of the canal. They were unbelievably dirty, which was not surprising in view of what they had been doing. The corporal was smoking a clay pipe. I indicated the lethal apparatus beside him. "Will it go off?" I enquired, "when we pull the plug?" "It might," said the corporal, "I've blown eight so far and all of them went off, but as the leads and charges have been under six inches of water since this morning I suppose it mightn't."'

The other two bridges were being prepared for demolition and Horsfall was worried they would not be ready in time. Refugees added confusion to the evaluation of defensive positions, but the throng moving north over the canal included some chance reinforcements.

'During the day quite a number of French soldiers came through us in small parties, often in twos and threes. These for the most part were not only good ones but very good indeed… One small formed body came in, a dozen of them under an adjutant chef. They were armed to the teeth with bandoliers slung about them, and they had a number of German weapons, including automatics. Most of them had bottles protruding from battle jacket pockets, and the overall impression was that of a party of pirates out on a shore raid.'

The chef asked Horsfall what his orders were. The reply was that they were to defend this place and, as regular soldiers, that is what they would do. It appealed to the Frenchman. He and his men would stay. It emerged that they had been made prisoner but had relieved their captors of their weapons and their lives and departed to rejoin the fight.

The canal itself was filled with sunken barges, so many that it seemed possible the Germans could walk across. Horsfall placed his men, had trenches dug, walls loopholed and reconnoitred the far bank. They were as ready as they ever would be. The next day German bombers, Stukas and Heinkels, attacked, but fortunately the other, southern, bank of the canal. The Faughs destroyed as many of the barges as they could both this day and the next, Thursday 23 May. Two French tanks, scarred by enemy fire, turned up and gladly took responsibility for the western flank. Their ammunition was low and the vacant shell racks were stocked with champagne. That evening the bridges were blown, the last of the battle-stained, French soldiers and the forward listening posts of the Faughs scampering back as the first of the Germans arrived. In Béthune the bridge went up with Germans on it, and three of the Fusiliers as well.

The 7th Panzer arrived next morning, apparently expecting no resistance. The contact with a regular regiment was a surprise for them and within a few hours there were dead and wounded Germans the length of the village street south of the water. The damage done by the Faughs in the isolated buildings at the waterside brought its penalty and by the end of the day the platoon had eight dead and only one bren gun still firing. The French tanks were also gone. They had driven up the ramp of the blown road bridge and subjected the Germans to a vicious fire until they themselves were hit. They were, Horsfall says, the last of their regiment and he grieved that he never knew which unit that was. On Saturday 25 May an ammunition train on the railway south of the canal blew up, wiping out the Germans who had been firing from between the wheels of the trucks, and giving some small respite to the Faughs. That same evening, to their puzzlement, they were relieved by the 1st/8th Lancashire Fusiliers of the 4th Brigade. The 50th Division was needed in the Ypres sector.

THE HALT ORDER

While the 1st Royal Irish Fusiliers might have been surprised to learn it, the two Panzer Corps had been ordered to halt on Friday 24 May. The impact of Frankforce's attack at Arras went all the way to the top, Hitler himself. Rundstedt and Kleist had both been worried about the exposure of their flanks, and Hitler shared their nervousness. The success they had enjoyed so far was almost too good to be true, and the blow delivered by a perceived five divisions on the previous Tuesday confirmed their fears. A French attack towards Cambrai on Wednesday, although turned back, reinforced their apprehensions. Moreover, the Luftwaffe's VIII Air Corps was now admitting to heavy Stuka losses inflicted by England-based RAF fighters.

The conclusion of the business in Flanders had not been planned in detail beforehand. Indeed, that they were here so soon was as much of a surprise to the Germans as it was to the Allies, and now the situation was that Army Group B was pressing from the north and east while Army Group A was applying pressure from the south and west on the remaining pocket of Allied troops. To whom should the control of the final phase be given? And which of the groups was best equipped for the task? The panzer-heavy Army Group A or the infantry-rich Army Group B? In the event the infantry of the 4th Army was taken from Rundstedt and placed under Bock's command in Army Group B. The concept then became one of infantry, artillery and air

power breaking the remainder of the Allies against the anvil of Army Group A holding a line from Gravelines through St Omer (i.e. along the river Aa) and on by way of Aire and Béthune to Lens (the Canal d'Aire or La Bassée line).

The nature of the terrain between Calais and Nieuport was well known to the Germans, and their maps and landscape assessments were uniform in their descriptions. The opinions of the generals at the front have been used to suggest that the terrain presented no problems for the panzers, but these generals themselves were to the rear. However, the evaluations were being made and the decisions were being taken by men far away, and they cannot but have been influenced by their official reference manuals and information sources. On 29 February 1940 a collection of maps and manuals was published in Berlin for the use of the services only. Volume I of *Militärgeographische Beschreibung von Frankreich* states that:

'In wet weather wide areas become boggy and impassable on foot. Vehicles can in general only move on the roads available which are very numerous and mostly fortified. These and the little railways run throughout on dykes; these form with the numerous, in general not very wide, water ways, canals and ditches a dense mesh of sections suitable for rearguard defence.'

The map that accompanies the manual, *Wehrgeolische Übersichtskarte,* (see p.93) comments on the terrain around Dunkirk:

'Predominant soil type: peat, groundwater near surface. Passability by traffic and on foot: At all times passable with difficulty. Accessible to infantry in dry season. Obstacles: Soft ground, criss-crossed with many ditches, shallow ground water, can be dug out to form water obstacles. Artillery firing positions: wet, ground not

MAIN PICTURE **Calais seen from the ridge just west of Guines. Assault Group Krüger came from the left along the road from which this photograph is taken and 3rd Royal Tanks came from Calais between the red-roofed farm and the woods to the right.**

(MME WW2/2/6)

able to take a load… Artillery observation opportunities: flat, low lying, without rises in ground.'

The land not actually shown as being below sea-level gets a rating only marginally better. This was the official assessment and it was relied upon. To men who had seen the torn landscapes of the previous war the message was obvious and inescapable; this land would be death to tanks with the first drop of rain.

Guderian was shocked. He wrote:

'On this day (the 24th) the Supreme Command intervened in the operations in progress, with results which were to have a most disastrous influence in the whole future course of the war. Hitler ordered the left wing to stop on the Aa. It was forbidden to cross that stream.'

Quoting from memory he went on to say that the order stated that Dunkirk was to be left to the Luftwaffe, as was Calais if it proved difficult to take.

'We were utterly speechless. But since we were not informed of the reasons for the order, it was difficult to argue against it. The panzer divisions were therefore instructed: "Hold the line of the canal. Make use of the period of rest for general recuperation."'

The SS Division Leibstandarte Adolf Hitler had been placed under Guderian's command and he ordered it to advance on Watten, six miles (10km) north of St Omer on the Aa. Early on the Saturday morning he went to check on them and discovered that the commander, Sepp Dietrich, had disobeyed the order, crossed the canalised river and taken position on the top of a hill amongst the ruins of a monastery. When Dietrich explained that, from the top of that hill, an enemy could look down the throat of his men on the western bank, Guderian agreed the position should be held.

By the time, on Sunday 26 May, Hitler gave the order to proceed once more, Boulogne had fallen, 2nd Panzer having finally breached the ancient walls with an 88mm flak gun. The 20th Guards Brigade had been ordered to evacuate the town by sea at 6.30 p.m. on Thursday 23 May and proceeded to do so without liaising with the French who had held on for another two days.

LEFT **The windmill at Watten with an unencumbered north view to Gravelines, given clear weather. This photograph was taken in June on a day when visibility was poor, much as it was in 1940. The ruined monastery is behind the wall to the right.**

(MME WW2/3/27)

THE SACRIFICE OF CALAIS'S DEFENDERS

On the same Thursday afternoon Assault Group Krüger of 1st Panzer was approaching the small town of Guines, on the ridge six miles (10km) south of Calais. The port itself was filled with newly-arrived troops, the 1st Queen Victoria's Rifles and the 3rd Royal Tank Regiment. The tanks were given orders by Lieutenant-general Sir Douglas Brownrigg, Gort's Adjutant-General, who was on his way to Dover, to make for Boulogne, but they were rescinded by Major Ken Bailey from Gort's headquarters. The instructions were now to head for St Omer. That proved to be impractical because Assault Group Krüger was making for Les Attaques, on the road to St Omer where the Canal de Calais runs beside the road, and 3rd Royal Tanks thus had a brief encounter with the panzers near Guines and had to withdraw. At Les Attaques an ad hoc force made up of Royal Artillery Searchlight personnel held up the panzers for three hours before being forced to surrender. Pushing up towards Calais Krüger ran into further opposition at Orphange Farm, just south of the present-day junction 17 on the autoroute. Here the fight continued until nightfall and at that point Guderian issued his order for 1st Panzer to push on towards Dunkirk and let 10th Panzer take over the conquest of Calais.

The forces in Calais were supplemented with 30th Brigade, 2nd King's Royal Rifle Corps (the Royal Green Jackets) and 1st, The Rifle Brigade, under the command of Brigadier Claude Nicholson, who arrived in the afternoon with renewed orders from Brownrigg to go for Boulogne. The Brigadier was bombarded with conflicting orders, all issued in ignorance of the actual state of affairs. Now directions from the War Office in London came to get rations through to

BELOW **The moat of the Citadel in Calais now has peaceful uses.** (MME WW2/2/5)

Gravelines. On the Thursday evening the supply convoy was readied to move off and an advance guard of a tank squadron sent ahead. It ran into 1st Panzer and only three tanks survived, fighting their way through to Gravelines. Having heard nothing, a second squadron was sent out the next morning, accompanied by a company of 1st Rifle Brigade. They, too, ran into the opposition and Nicholson ordered them to come back. Calais was isolated.

Nicholson now readied his forces and the 800 French to defend the town. The walls and bastions of Vauban's 17th-century defences were still in place and still formidable. Within a double ring of defensive positions he could fall back on the harbour for eventual evacuation, a scheme approved in principle by London. The wounded and the 'useless mouths', a rather unkind description of anyone not vital for combat, were leaving. The *City of Canterbury* took with it, through confusion or oversight, half the Rifle Brigade transport. The last vessel to leave, the *Kohistan*, was watched by a young troop commander of the Searchlights, Airey Neave.

'Calais had become a city of doom and I was not in the least anxious to remain. I did not feel heroic. Leaving the men, sleepless and anxious, I walked to the Gare Maritime in time to see the Kohistan *leave harbour. The quay was deserted save for the twenty dead on the platform. The scene remains vivid. It was a clear day and I could see the cliffs of Dover. The sad corpses, covered in grey blankets, had begun to stink. Shells burst among the cranes or landed in the sea. A mile out, the destroyer* Wessex, *struck by Luftwaffe bombs, was sinking. Black smoke from the blazing oil refinery billowed across the harbour and, to the west and south of town, there came the growing noise of rifle and anti-tank fire. The real battle was about to begin.'*

That evening the Brigadier received a signal from London informing him that he was under the command of General Falgade, who forbade their evacuation. Churchill added his more positive encouragement and Anthony Eden edited and sent the message the next day:

'Defence of Calais to the utmost is of highest importance to our country as symbolising our continued co-operation with France. The eyes of the Empire are upon the defence of Calais, and H. M. Government are confident you and your gallant regiments will perform an exploit worthy of the British name.'

The outer perimeter was the scene of action on Friday 24 May. Neave was on the Boulevard Léon Gambetta which passes just north of Bastion 9 of Vauban's fortification, running west. His unit had two bren guns as their most powerful weapons and held out there all day. As afternoon turned to evening, it became clear that the outer defences could not endure. Nicholson and the French Commandant Le Tellier had established their headquarters in the Citadel

LEFT **Calais – composite of two German 1:25,000 maps made after the occupation. The lines of the old walls and bastions can be traced from Bastion 2, right of the harbour, then running south past Bastions 3, 4, 5 and 6 at the south-eastern corner and 7 at the southern tip. Bastion 8 has gone, replaced by the railway, and, going north, 9, 10, 11 form the western wall with the citadel within. Fort Nieulay dominates the western approaches. To the south-west rises the ridge on which Guines stands and east of it the country is heavily patterned with drainage dykes.** (BL C21 (15), sheets XXII-2/5-6 and 8/3-4)

which was the centre of the western flank. The withdrawal brought the 60th Rifles back from Bastion 9 in the west and Bastion 7 in the south (Bastion 8 no longer existed in 1940) towards the Hôtel de Ville. The QVR were pulled in from their positions on the Gravelines road. Snipers within the town hampered British movement. By midnight most of the defenders were getting what rest they could in position for the expected onslaught on Sunday 26 May. Bastion 11 to the north-west was held and a line along the waterways embraced the Citadel, passed north of the Hôtel de Ville and swung round towards the Gare Maritime and Bastion 1 at the harbour mouth.

Sunday began badly. The shelling was intense and the dive-bombing even more fierce. At 8 a.m. a white flag was seen above French positions near Fort Risban, west of the harbour. Capitaine de Frégate Carlos de Lambertye, commander of French naval forces in Calais, went and persuaded them to take it down, but renewed shelling made them raise it once more. Later that morning, making his way to Fort Risban, de Lambertye collapsed and died of a heart attack. By mid-morning the Germans had occupied Bastion 2 at the extreme north-east and were firing on the Rifle Brigade. Neave had been wounded and treated at the Hôpital Militaire near the Citadel. He left to find

ABOVE **From within the Citadel the harbour can be seen.** (MME WW2/2/4)

RIGHT **A memorial plaque to the 110th Regiment inside the Citadel gate.** (MME WW2/2/1)

transport to move the wounded to the harbour where he believed they could be shipped out. Accompanied by a corporal, Neave wandered through an empty town.

'Opposite a whole row of houses burned. Charred paper blew like leaves along the narrow street. We walked slowly northwards... Then, without warning, shells whistled and burst near us ... The corporal vanished in the blinding flash and dust. I fell to the ground unhurt and crawled to the side of the street where a hand streched out from a cellar window, holding a bottle of cognac. I drank from it and staggered on towards the lighthouse.'

At the swing bridge to the Gare Maritime he was faced with the muzzles of the QVR's rifles and tottered on into their arms. His suggestion that they send transport, clearly completely impossible, was regarded as very odd and he was hustled along to join the other wounded in the tunnel below Bastion 1.

Major-general Ferdinand Schaal, commander of 10th Panzer Division, had planned the day's activities with care. Two bouts of shelling and bombing were to give him the town before noon. It proved to be a little more difficult. They had entered Calais Nord late in the morning, but the fragmented groups of British fought stubbornly on. At Bastion 11 C Company, 60th Rifles and the few Frenchman who had fought alongside them so bravely were virtually isolated by mid-day, and withdrew, leaving some 80 men under Captain Everard Radcliffe there to cover their retreat. It was another hour before the Germans entered the bastion to take prisoner the 17 surviving Frenchmen and the rump of C Company, of whom only 30 were unwounded. There was no resistance; there was no ammunition.

German anger and frustration mounted. Schaal received repeated messages to leave the job to the Luftwaffe, but his blood was up. Stukas struck again and again and the shelling redoubled. As day crept into afternoon the Gare Maritime was threatened and the Germans only had the two bastions on the east of the harbour mouth to overcome. The conflict moved into the sand dunes. In the Citadel the Royal Marines and Le Tellier's troops were still defying their attackers. By 3 p.m. they were surrounded and, half an hour later, the Germans broke through the southern gate and Nicholson had no alternative to surrender. It was to be another two hours before all resistance ceased. At 2a.m. on Monday 27 May, HM Yacht *Gulzar*, Lieutenant-commander Brammall commanding, saw a signal lamp flashing from beneath a German-occupied jetty. She went in and as she swung round under machine-gun fire, Brammall shouted that he would come in again and they would have to jump. All 47 men made it, the last men out. There were 3,000 British and 800 French troops who were not so fortunate.

The sacrifice at Calais had been costly for the British, reducing still further the number of regular soldiers available. It had resulted in sufficient delay for Hitler's halt order to catch 1st Panzer well short of Gravelines and allow two days for the BEF to begin the complicated task of maintaining a shrinking front. The Belgians were close to collapse, the French 7th Army south of the Somme seemed to be a myth and the task that Gort now faced was to preserve what he could of the BEF to fight another day. It was a task that would demand all his courage and steadfastness, attributes that few other men could match.

DYNAMO

During the two days the halt order was in force, events were also unfolding away from the Channel coast. Lord Gort and General Pownall visited Blanchard on Sunday 26 May to find the plan was now to defend the salient based on the Channel coast 'with no thought of retreat'. On returning to his headquarters Gort found a message from London saying that should the planned attack from the south fail to materialise, the safety of the BEF would become the predominant consideration and a withdrawal to the coast east of Gravelines for embarkation should be planned. He was further instructed not to discuss the matter with the Belgians or the French.

On 14 May a call had been broadcast, nothing to do with a possible evacuation of the BEF, for small boats to supplement the Royal Navy's Small Vessels Pool, little ships useful for harbour work. When Vice-Admiral Bertram Ramsay was appointed on 19 May to make plans for a possible evacuation, some of those little ships were already becoming available. His early plans were based on the use of Boulogne, Calais and Dunkirk, but by the time the meeting of Wednesday 22 May took place, only four days into the task, it was evident that only Dunkirk, and that with luck, would be spared. Operation Dynamo, as it was called, was turning out to be more complicated than anticipated. Ramsay had originally been given three dozen cross-channel steamers for the task which was to begin with lifting the useless mouths, support troops. Now the intensity was increasing exponentially, the need for additional staff had to be met to handle the operation and many, many more ships were going to be needed. Churchill, when evacuation became inevitable, thought that, perhaps, 30,000 men could be saved. Ramsay was more optimistic, maybe 45,000 could be brought home. The difficulties were enormous, not the least in the nature of the coast. East of the Margate-Dover coast the Goodwin Sands run from north to south, forcing ships to sail in the direction of

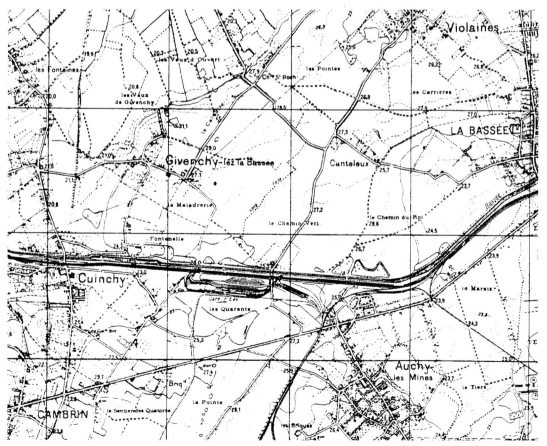

LEFT **Detail from a German map of the Canal d'Aire (La Bassée Canal) between Cuinchy and La Bassée. The Gare d'Eau, the harbour in which 7th Panzer's engineers worked on pontoons, is east of Cuinchy.** (BL C21 (15), sheet XXIV-5/3-4. MME WW2Maps/3/35)

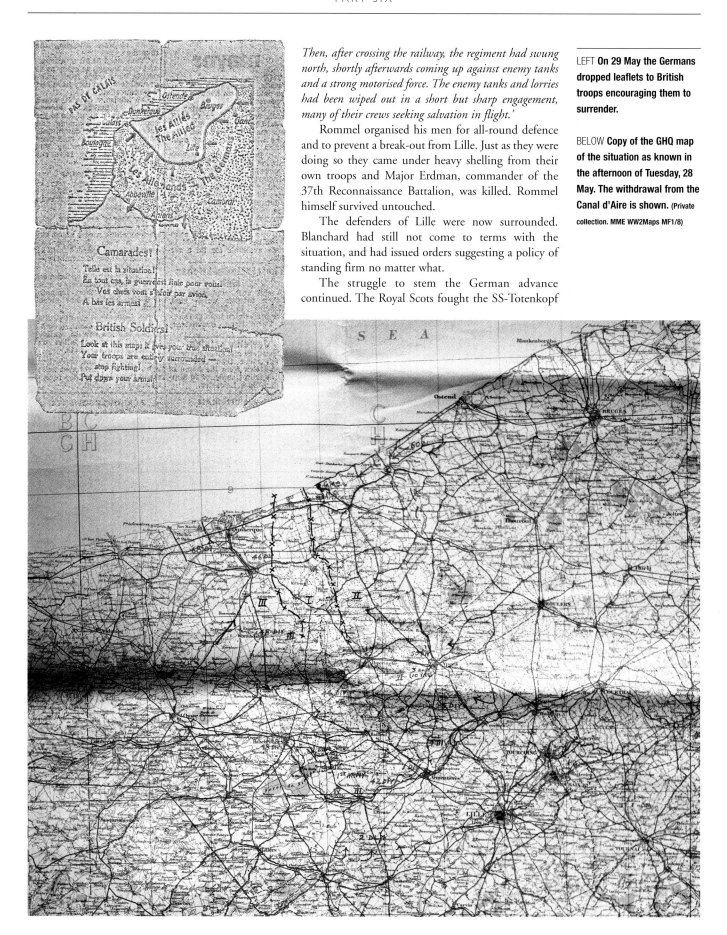

Then, after crossing the railway, the regiment had swung north, shortly afterwards coming up against enemy tanks and a strong motorised force. The enemy tanks and lorries had been wiped out in a short but sharp engagement, many of their crews seeking salvation in flight.'

Rommel organised his men for all-round defence and to prevent a break-out from Lille. Just as they were doing so they came under heavy shelling from their own troops and Major Erdman, commander of the 37th Reconnaissance Battalion, was killed. Rommel himself survived untouched.

The defenders of Lille were now surrounded. Blanchard had still not come to terms with the situation, and had issued orders suggesting a policy of standing firm no matter what.

The struggle to stem the German advance continued. The Royal Scots fought the SS-Totenkopf

LEFT **On 29 May the Germans dropped leaflets to British troops encouraging them to surrender.**

BELOW **Copy of the GHQ map of the situation as known in the afternoon of Tuesday, 28 May. The withdrawal from the Canal d'Aire is shown.** (Private collection. MME WW2Maps MF1/8)

Division at Paradis and the last of those British troops fell back to Lestrem where the Irish Fusiliers were holding the line of the little river over which three bridges passed. John Horsfall took a look at the country before him.

'I went into the estaminet [bar] and up to the first floor. The countryside to the west looked quiet enough, and save for the hum of aircraft there was not a lot of noise just then. However looking through my field glasses, as far as one could see westward the glinting reflection from turret tops and other impedimenta told their tale unmistakably.'

They had two 18-pounders dug in alongside the bridge. This stuck out like the cherry on a cake from the semi-circle of river that ran round the town, and Horsfall had to send out parties to guard his flanks. Various fragments of Allied soldiery straggled in.

'Finally to my great delight my old friend the adjutant chef and a number of our devoted allies from Gorre arrived. There were not many of them left – perhaps eight or so… There was much hilarity and shaking of hands, and all were loaded with bottles. Also, as previously, they were armed to the teeth with British, French – and German weapons.'

As at Gorre, Horsfall consulted the sappers and checked the arrangements to blow the bridges. The French engineers had a cheerful disregard for formal safety procedures.

'"It is quite all right, Capitaine," said one of them, pointing to the plunger, "if that fails we have les autres. That one, ici," he went on, indicating a pair of fuses whose colour I forget, "is instamment, vite très vite, and the other deux minutes," or whatever. He held up his fingers like Winston's V-sign. It was no doubt a great misunderstanding… An hour later a warrant officer and a dozen or so men of the Royal Scots plunged into

the dyke … and swam the river with the enemy hard on their heels.'

The 18-pounders may have lacked sights, but the gunners managed to bring down a surprisingly accurate fire on the tanks while the German infantry, at first, advanced with their rifles at the high port as if on some parade ground. The Faugh's precise rifle fire soon discouraged them. Horsfall decided it was time to blow the bridge. The plunger was pushed home.

'The silence that followed was a spiritual purgative, and I know of no comparable anti-climax in the whole of my life. I looked stonily at our French friend. He looked at me too – by no means abashed… I lit the match and applied it to the deux minutes one [fuse]. Of course the bridge went up instamment … The French thought it a huge joke.'

As evening approached the Faughs were withdrawn. They fired off the last of the 18-pounder

ABOVE **Even when surrounded the French held on in Lille, forcing the Germans to fight their way into the town.** (TM 4506/B/4)

BELOW LEFT **The memorial to the 97 massacred prisoners-of-war in Le Paradis.** (MME WW2/3/36)

BELOW RIGHT **At the side of the D17 from Wormhout to Esquelbecq stands a memorial to the Warwicks, Cheshires and Gunners slaughtered near here on 28 May 1940.** (MME WW2/3/13)

RIGHT and BELOW **General Alfred Wäger** did the French the honour of allowing them to march past while he and his staff saluted their courage, before they finally laid down their arms.

(B126/311/4 and B126/311/13)

ammunition, saving the last two rounds of each gun for the classic one shell down in the muzzle, the other in the breech final shot. The adjutant chef and his men declined to come along. They said their wish was to kill Germans and this appeared to be a good place for it. Horsfall paid his respects and left.

Behind them, in Lille, the French 1st Army had continued to fight, surrounded though it was. After four days they had no more ammunition with which to continue their resistance and were forced to yield on 1 June. Such was the respect they had earned that they were accorded full military honours, retaining their arms in their final march. Some 35,000 men went into captivity.

BACKS TO THE SEA

While Gort, his plea to Blanchard to order General Prioux to retreat from Lille falling on deaf ears, hastened his men back towards the sea, the leaders of France were conferring in Paris. It was becoming clear to them at last that they faced disaster. The knowledge failed to harden their resolve. Increasingly there was thought of an armistice as long as the honour of France could be kept intact.

On Tuesday 28 May Gort's headquarters were established at La Panne, bringing him, technically, under the command of Admiral Jean Abrial, commanding officer in Dunkirk. It was something of a formality. Weygand was still insisting that the Dunkirk salient should be defended as a bridgehead from which a counter-attack could be launched. It was a fantasy. Re-supply of weapons and ammunition, fuel and food was clearly impossible, but the fantasy

persisted and led to innumerable disputes as the British destroyed equipment lest the enemy acquire it and the French preserved as much as they could for supposed future use.

The evacuation was slowly gathering momentum. Churchill informed Reynaud of British intentions and urged him to issue corresponding orders. Sadly the French Prime Minister appears to have kept the news to himself, another source of enmity between the Allies. On the first day, Sunday 26 May, Operation Dynamo was put into action at 6.57 p.m. and a few

ABOVE **An AFV makes short work of a sandbag obstacle.** (TM 4505/E/5)

LEFT **Bombing reduced towns on the retreat route to blazing ruins.** (TM 4505/F/4)

men were brought home. These had all been embarked from Dunkirk harbour, as were those taken off on Monday, 7,669 men according to Churchill's history of the war, but bombing, shelling as the ships sailed along the coast inside the sandbanks and strafing by the Luftwaffe as they turned out across the Channel had inflicted casualties. A meeting in Cassel on Monday led to Lieutenant-general Sir Robert Adam and General Fagalde sorting out the French and British sectors of the planned perimeter; the French on the west and the British on the east. As no one seemed to know what was happening to the Belgians, no provision was made for them and, in any case, they capitulated the following day, though not without providing for the British to take over their positions.

On Thursday 23 May Commander TGP Crick, RN, had been woken at 4 a.m. and told to hold himself in readiness for an appointment. At 6.30 he

was summoned to a meeting and ordered to take command of a Dutch barge, a 'scoot' as the English mangled the word *schuit*, and take supplies to Dunkirk. With a first lieutenant and a crew of nine he went to the port, not named in his account, and sent the Dutch crew ashore before loading with ammunition. At 7.30 p.m. on Sunday they moved to Dover and crossed the Channel the next night, arriving at 5 a.m. on Tuesday 28 May at La Panne. There was an almost empty beach before him, just a few French and Belgian soldiers. Wandering into La Panne he found his way to the Hotel Osborne where the English-speaking manager directed him to the British hospital. There he learnt that an evacuation was taking place and was sent on once more to BEF headquarters. The ammunition was not needed, but the boat was, to get men off the beach. So back he went to the vessel, now high and dry, to unload under fire from German aircraft and to get men organised to go aboard when the tide came in at 5.30 p.m. Commander Crick did get home, but not on that boat. During the afternoon he was hit when the beach was strafed, the ammunition luckily going unscathed, and he was evacuated from Dunkirk, leaving his ship to bring men home without him.

Ramsay had acquired a fleet of about 50 Dutch *schuitjes*, self-propelled shallow-draught cargo barges that had managed to get away from the Netherlands and were lying at Southampton. Although some of these were already involved in the operation on Tuesday 28 May, the destroyers that Ramsay had managed to bring in had to use their own boats to get men off the beaches. The day's totals were 5,930 men taken off the beaches and 11,874 from Dunkirk. The lack of discipline on the beaches and at the port did not help. The word was now going out for small ships of any description to join the evacuation effort. Sailing barges, pleasure steamers and fishing boats were

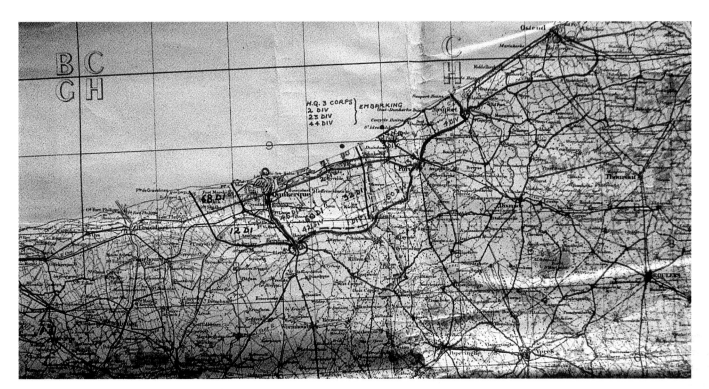

requisitioned or volunteered. On Wednesday 29 May the beaches yielded up 13,752 and Dunkirk 33,558 men, still all British. That afternoon, at last, Weygand ordered Blanchard to get his men away as well.

Reichsmarchall Herman Göring's undertaking to reduce the Dunkirk enclave from the air was slow in execution. There was little air activity on Sunday 26 May, although the RAF flew 22 patrols and claimed, no doubt exaggerated as all such claims were, 20 victories for a loss of six machines. On Monday the Luftwaffe went to work in earnest. Heinkel 111s raided at dawn, sinking the French steamer *Aden* by the east mole in Dunkirk and shortly after Junkers 87s, the Stukas, hit the harbour and sank the troopship *Côte d'Azur*. Dornier 17s set the oil tanks on fire. Some 300 bombers, escorted by 550 fighters, attacked Dunkirk that day, turning the town into a lake of fire and blocking the port. The RAF had not been idle, flying 23 patrols involving 287 aircraft and scoring some successes, but a significant proportion of British aircraft were badly damaged in addition to those shot down. Tuesday 28 May brought a break in the fine weather. Overcast skies, coupled with the smoke from the ruins of Dunkirk, produced adverse flying conditions which persisted the next day until early afternoon. Then the Stukas returned in force, 180 of them, closing the harbour again, although losing 11 aircraft to anti-aircraft fire. The next wave included Junkers 88s, the twin-engined dive-bombers, and three British destroyers were sunk. Five transport vessels also went down that Wednesday. Of the five major German attacks only two were met by RAF fighters and, although exotic claims were made of 65

RIGHT **As the weather deteriorated, off-road conditions became impossible for heavy vehicles.** (TM 5787/A3)

BELOW **The memorial to the French 12th Motorised Infantry on the front at Bray-Dunes with Dunkirk beyond.** (MME WW2/2/12)

kills, the true total appears to be closer to a dozen. Flying at something close to the limits of their operational range and even assisted, as they were, by radar in England, the British aircraft were simply outnumbered by the covering German fighters when the weather was clear. What was needed was fog.

Inland the Allies were still trying to cling on to positions of vantage. The Mont des Cats was the destination to which 1/5th Queen's were ordered on the evening of Tuesday 28 May. They were disappointed, for they felt they had given their enemies a bloody nose in hard fighting near Strazeele, between Hazebrouck and Bailleul that day, and Sysonby wrote:

'*I had only just gone to sleep from sheer exhaustion on*

a pile of straw when I was woken and given a message. It was then 10 o'clock p.m. and the message said that we were to withdraw at once and leave all transport behind us. This was a very bitter blow as for one thing we were all convinced that we had given the Germans a really good hiding ... We marched through the lines and had an uneventful march of about seven miles [11km] ... the road was choked with transport ... When we had climbed the hill we were bound for we just fell down where we stood and went to sleep in the open and in the rain.'

The 2nd Royal Horse Artillery were ordered to the same place and by the early hours of Tuesday 29 May, Seton-Watson writes,

'*... we started our move northwards, interweaving with every kind of British and French vehicle and many loose horses. After two miles we found our road blocked by ditched and abandoned vehicles. With great difficulty we constructed a detour through cut wire and hedges and across two fields: this took about an hour. At 0300 [3.a.m.] in the small village of Berthem, close under Mont des Cats, we came to a final standstill... Orders were given to destroy wireless sets and sights, remove breech blocks and puncture all tyres. It was impossible to destroy the guns themselves without danger to the crowds passing by on foot.*'

When Sysonby awoke at 3.30 a.m. a French officer told him, as a matter of apparently mild interest, that everyone else had gone. 1/5th Queen's awaited orders, shelled, dive-bombed and defenceless against such attack. At 9.45 a.m. they were told to pull out and make for Dunkirk by way of Poperinge. Sysonby said:

'*... the place was in the most appalling shambles. Whole streets were completely choked with masonry and* *bricks, anything up to twenty feet [6m] high. They must have taken the most appalling bombardment the night before ... even whilst we were here this place took another terrible pasting ...'*

They struggled on, taking avoiding action and turning north across country when German troops were reported ahead. Finally they reached the Canal de la Basse Colme east of the walled town of Bergues, the final line of defence. Over that and onwards they plodded to a final halt and blessed sleep at Uxen, five miles (8km) east of Dunkirk. It was a journey typical of thousands.

THE GREAT ESCAPE

On Tuesday 28 May Guderian made a tour of his forward positions, according to his unit's war diary, though he fails to mention it in his memoirs. He reported to the Chief of Staff, Kleist Group, that only half of the panzers remained operational and that repairs and renewals were vital. Further, he said:

'A tank attack is pointless in the marshy country which has been completely soaked by the rain... 18 Army [of Army Group B] is approaching ... from the east. The infantry forces of this army are more suitable than tanks for fighting in this kind of country, and the task of closing the gap on the coast can therefore be left to them.'

It appears that the caution of the High Command was not misplaced in preventing a panzer advance four days previously. The panzer divisions were withdrawn from the front.

Within the beachhead some system was now introduced. Rear-Admiral W. F. Wake-Walker arrived on the morning of Thursday 30 May to take command of the beach operation. The day was foggy and a steady rain

LEFT **A plaque on the Bray-Dunes monument commemorates a lost ship.** (MME WW2/2/14)

BELOW **The French fallen are commemorated close to the Fort des Dunes at Leffrinckoucke.** (MME WW2/2/32)

fell; miserable weather for the huddled men on the beaches, and impossible weather for the Luftwaffe. The scene that greeted Wake-Walker differed entirely from the plans he had been shown in Dover, the three neat beaches, Malo-les-Bains, Bray-Dunes and La Panne, each sub-divided into tidy administrative sections. The beaches were thronged with men, long lines curving into the water where they stood waiting for small boats to lift them out. There were too few small boats. Repeated appeals were made to Dover by Wake-Walker and others. As they day wore on the calm Channel became dotted with flocks of little vessels, pleasure steamers, yachts, sailing barges, all making their way towards the

cauldron of the beaches. To facilitate embarkation jetties of lorries were built out into the sea. On 30 May the total lifted from the beaches rose to 29,512, more than double the day before. The bulk of the evacuations was, throughout the operation, from the east mole, the long, narrow, man-made spit of concrete that sheltered Dunkirk harbour from easterly seas. The damage done by bombers the day before slowed things on this Thursday, only 24,311 men left, but work was in hand to move damaged vessels and repair the shattered walkway out to a point where large ships could dock.

The 1/5th Queen's reached Malo-les-Bains on Thursday morning and moved forward towards the sea as evening came. Sysonby described the procedure.

'*The men were divided into parties of fifty and each given a serial number, ours being 142. A somewhat primitive movement control was established on the knoll [mole]. As the numbers were called out the party shot forward through the dirty sand and marched along the knoll. The shelling was increasing and the Germans were getting the range more accurately. Luckily they were concentrating their efforts on the inner harbour and I saw one shell strike a ship absolutely amidships. As we were marching down the knoll we saw the bodies of four British soldiers lying there covered with greatcoats. It was very tragic they had got so far and near to safety. We arrived at the end of the knoll and saw a magnificent naval officer [possibly Commander Campbell Clouston] standing there in blue uniform with a walking stick, completely unruffled by the shelling that was going on all round him. He called out "Round the corner and a smart*

LEFT **Fine weather for an evacuation. In the middle of a June morning there is no chance of seeing Dunkirk from the height of Mont Cassel.** (MME WW2/3/20)

RIGHT **The Fort des Dunes at Leffrinckoucke was stubbornly defended by the French as some of their comrades took to the ships with the British.** (MME WW2/2/28)

FAR RIGHT **The Fort was to see more French lives sacrificed before the war was over.**
(MME WW2/2/25)

double for two hundred yards [180m]." With that we set off … It was then pretty dark and there were no gangways to the ships … We had to slide across a plank two feet wide and walk down a rather sharp incline to the ship. It is a thing I could not have done normally but I was so anxious to get out of this foul place. The ships were absolutely packed out … as we steamed down the channel for an hour we were still in range of the German artillery which, however, was firing very wildly … We landed at about 0700 at Folkestone… We went … to a little village in Gloucestershire called Wickwar … they allowed us to sleep for as long as we wanted to.'

For men on the beaches matters were less certain. Alwyn Ward was serving with 9th Army Field Workshop, Royal Army Ordnance Corps. His unit had come back through Bergues and, on Tuesday 28 May, marched into Bray-Dunes. There some happily helped themselves to unguarded bottles of wine, while others used a hammer to inflict war-like dents in their helmets to impress the folks back home. They were then ordered into the sand dunes to await their turn to embark, and there, exhausted, they slept soundly in the drizzle. Wednesday found them still waiting their turn and, two by two, they were allowed to go and look around. Ward writes:

'When we reached the beach, I was struck by the great change in the situation compared with what we had seen the previous evening. There were many more ships off shore, and plenty of small boats embarking troops. I noticed there were hardly any large groups of men standing around aimlessly waiting to be told what to do… We walked until our way was blocked by a wide

RIGHT **Stranded boats and
abandoned vehicles littered
the beach and shallows at
Malo-les-Bains. The Dunkirk
mole is in the distance.**
(B75/18/34)

BELOW **The shore between the
West Bastion at Dunkirk and
Zuydcoote, from German
maps. From Malo-les-Bains
the mole reached out to the
west and to the east, beyond
Malo Terminus, is Fort des
Dunes and, on the sea-front,
the Zuydcoote Sanitorium.
The extent of the dunes is
clear to see.** (BL C21 (15) sheets
XXIII-2/1-2 and 3-4)

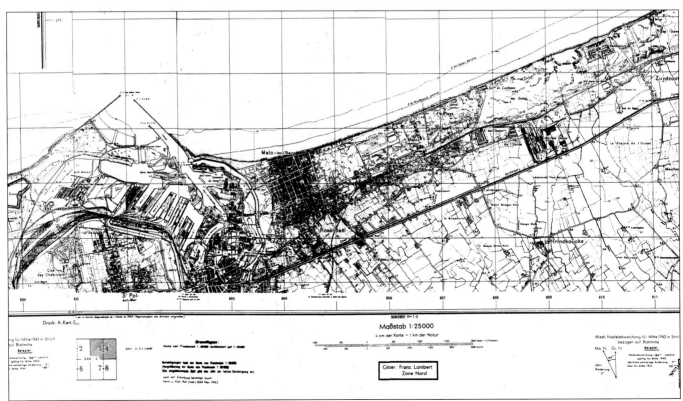

queue… Its length was so enormous, and the pace of lifting troops into the boats was so slow, it would be ages before those at the rear end were embarked.'

They were moved on to Zuydcoote on Wednesday and there settled down once more to wait for the order to join a queue. A holiday spirit prevailed, water was found, a little food was foraged and songs were sung.

'Despite the slow process of lifting men into the boats, the queues moved steadily forward, and there was plenty of laughing and joking going on… I never actually noticed the changing weather pattern and that the visibility had improved. One moment we were singing away… the next moment all hell was let loose around us.'

The bombers dived and turned with relentless efficiency. Ward and his companions were relatively safe in the dunes, but still suffered casualties. That evening they were moved again, to Malo-les-Bains, where, two days later, they finally left from the mole.

The experience of the mariners coming to the rescue was equally memorable. A. D. Divine wrote:

'The picture will always remain sharp-etched in my memory – the lines of men wearily and sleepily staggering across the beach from the dunes to the shallows, falling into little boats; great columns of men thrust out into the water among bomb and shell splashes. The foremost ranks were shoulder deep … As the front ranks were dragged aboard the boats, the rear ranks moved up, from ankle deep to knee deep, from knee deep to waist deep, until they, too, came to shoulder depth and their turn … And always down the dunes and across the beach came new hordes of men, new columns, new lines … There was always the red background, the red of Dunkirk

burning … The din was infernal. The batteries shelled ceaselessly and brilliantly. To the whistle of shells overhead was added the scream of falling bombs. Even the sky was full of noise – anti-aircraft shells, machine-gun fire, the snarl of falling planes, the angry hornet noise of dive bombers. One could not speak normally at any time against the roar of it and the noise of our own engines.'

The British were getting off, but the French were less fortunate. The British, from the Commander-in-Chief downwards, assumed that the evacuation of the BEF was their priority and their orders from London appeared to confirm this. Indeed, when the first troops were leaving Dunkirk the French were expressly charged by Weygand to hold their ground preliminary to a counter-attack and they were unaware that their allies had already started to leave. When Admiral Wake-Walker arrived he was under instructions from the First Sea Lord to refuse the French places on the ships if there were British troops ready to depart but the next day Churchill was, at a meeting in Paris, declaring that the Allies should leave arm-in-arm. Lord Gort was beset with the problem of whom should be left behind if now French and British were to be shipped out in equal numbers, but the problem soon ceased to be his. On Friday 31 May he handed over command to Major-general Harold Alexander and reluctantly obeyed his orders to return to England. Alexander's orders from London specified withdrawal '50/50' with the French. Admiral Abrial had no choice but to concur with his subordinate, the line would be held until midnight on 1 June and the last departures would take place on Sunday 2 June.

BELOW **The memorial at Malo-les-Bains.** (MME WW2/2/33)

RIGHT **The memorial window at the CWGC Cemetery, Dunkirk.** (MME WW2/3/1)

BELOW **Crowded graves in the CWGC Cemetery, Dunkirk.** (MME WW2/3/2)

The air battle resumed with the improvement in the weather on Friday 31 May. Three raids by Heinkels and Dorniers sank one ship and damaged others at a cost, by the Luftwaffe's figures, of 17 machines. The RAF flew not only fighter sorties but also missions to strike at German ground forces, losing 28 aircraft in all. The beautiful weather of Saturday 1 June combined with the dwindling resources of the RAF to allow heavy air raids on the beach-head and the next day German daylight reconnaissance reported an almost empty sea, for what movement was left was undertaken by night. During Operation Dynamo the RAF lost 177 aircraft of which 107 were fighters. Luftwaffe losses, according to their own figures, came to 132 at Dunkirk and 108 in other areas. For the first time in this war Göring had encountered serious opposition.

THE FINAL PHASE

Friday 31 May saw the peak performance in terms of numbers of men embarked. There were 22,942 taken off the beaches and 45,072 from the mole. By Saturday morning some 39,000 British were within the perimeter and about 50,000 French were forming the rearguard with the same number in readiness to leave. Only 15,000 Frenchman had been taken off previously. The air raids, facing reduced opposition, did great damage. Three British and one French

destroyers were sunk, together with four minesweepers and two transport ships. None the less the previous day's total was nearly equalled, 17,348 left the beaches and 47,081 the mole. Further losses were reduced by operating at night and the final lift was planned for the night of Saturday to Sunday. The operations did not go as planned and some ships returned empty while numbers of French troops sought vainly their embarkation points. On Sunday and Monday nights the ships returned and did somewhat better, the totals for the last three days coming to 26,256, 26,745 and 26,175 respectively. Admiral Abrial came out with the final group and, when Admiral Ramsay enquired about trying one more time the next night, he had to decline the offer; the beach-head was now in German hands. The formal surrender of the remaining troops took place on Tuesday 4 June.

The German failure to wipe out, by killing or capturing, the BEF and the French 1st Army was to cost them dear. A nucleus of British forces, 198,315 men, had been preserved for the future. Their Allies, mostly French, had 139,911 taken off, but most of the French returned to their own country by way of Cherbourg to continue the immediate battle. It had been a remarkable achievement, but as Churchill remarked, wars are not won by evacuations. And the Battle of France was not over yet.

LEFT **French dead of 1940 lie at Leffrinckoucke.** (MME WW2/2/24)

BELOW **French prisoners are kept under observation on the quayside at Dunkirk.** (B71/86/6)

LEFT **Mounted German support troops arriving at Dunkirk weeks later see the evidence of a massive surrender.** (TM 5787/A4)

FROM THE SOMME TO THE SEINE

Orders were given by Hitler on 28 May for the formation of a Panzer Group under the command of Guderian. On 1 June he established his headquarters at Signy-le-Petit, south-west of Charleville where he had been only a short while before, and set about assembling his new command. On Tuesday 4 June Rommel and 7th Panzer were moving south towards the Somme to take part in the next phase of the conquest of France, Fall Rot, Operation Red. The orders for the destruction of the Allies south of the Somme and the Aisne were issued on Friday 31 May. The west, from the Channel to Reims, would be taken by Army Group B while the east, from Reims to the Maginot Line, was the sector of Army Group A, leaving Army Group C in its former position facing the Maginot Line from the north. Only one fort of that line, at La Ferté, had been attacked and taken by the Germans. The rest would be left to surrender when all else had fallen.

General Weygand had 60 divisions with which to face the 143 the Germans devoted to the operation. These had, in part, come from a thinning of the

LEFT **The fort at the extreme west of the Maginot Line, Villy la Ferté, was overcome by the Germans on 19 May.**
(MME WW2/6/22 or 23)

ABOVE **A diagram of the action that led to the fall of Villy la Ferté commemorates the French defence.**
(MME WW2/6/26)

ABOVE **From the height of the Monts de Caubert the country to the south is easy to observe.** (MME Mon/Diep98/1/20)

RIGHT **British armour on the move in Quesnoy, south of the Somme and west of Abbeville, in May 1940.**
(IWM F4600)

Maginot Line forces as well as what reserves were available, now 15 divisions, ten having been deployed in May, and there were elements of sound fighting forces rescued from Dunkirk. The tactical approach was changed. Orders were given for selected strong points to be defended with vigour and even to persist when surrounded. The troops would then break out when the main danger had passed, or the special shock troops being held in reserve would act to relieve them. Unfortunately the organisation of forces in the new formations necessary to realise the scheme demanded time, and that is what the Germans denied him. In the west they were already in possession of bridgeheads at Abbeville, Amiens and Péronne. From the first two towns the two Panzer Divisions of Gruppe Hoth would strike towards the Seine while Gruppe von Kleist from Péronne would go for the Marne. East of Reims Gruppe Guderian would spearhead the advance. As a preliminary Paris was bombed on 3 June.

REGAINING THE SOMME BRIDGEHEADS

While the eyes of the world had been on the retreat to Dunkirk and the evacuation of the allied armies, efforts were being made to challenge the German presence in the Somme bridgeheads. Elements of 1st Armoured had taken part in ill-directed forays west of Amiens on 23 and 24 May in support of a supposed attack by the French 7th Army. The intelligence about the bridges still intact was faulty and most of the planned rendezvous failed to materialise. This was the basis of the belief that a major attack from the south would cut off the panzers from the rest of the German forces. On Saturday 25 May Major-general Roger Evans was told his 1st Armoured was now to come

under the command of General Robert Altmayer, brother of René, who headed a new formation, *Groupement A*, which soon became the 10th Army. The first task Altmayer undertook was to eliminate the Abbeville bridgehead. Evans pointed out that his division could not spearhead the operation as his tanks were light cruisers, intended for open country, high-speed actions and insufficiently armoured for the task. The objection was treated as trivial.

On Sunday the French 7th Army's attacks were halted, one south of Abbeville at Huppy, the other at Dury, south of Amiens. On Monday the British 2nd Armoured Brigade went for Huppy, together with the French 2nd Light Cavalry. The attack was poorly co-ordinated and the British found themselves going it alone. The 10th Hussars lost 20 tanks before withdrawing. The Queen's Bays to their right fared a little better, losing only 12 tanks. Added to the losses

ABOVE **The French memorial on the Monts de Caubert. The concrete dome to the left is the remains of the First World War memorial in the form of a French helmet. The hillock on the skyline is surmounted with German gun emplacements.**
(MME Mon/Diep98/1/21)

LEFT **A lonely monument to French fallen stands at the roadside between Cambron and Lambercourt.**
(MME Mon/Diep98/1/23)

of the few days before, the Brigade was approaching exhaustion of its AFVs. The 3rd Armoured and the 5th Light Cavalry were operating further west. They managed to reach the high ground south of the Somme and, at the extreme left, the outskirts of St Valery-sur-Somme on the estuary itself, but supporting French infantry was slow in following up the gains and they were forced to fall back. In all the British lost 65 tanks that day and a further 50 were in need of repair before coming back into service.

Charles de Gaulle was promoted Brigadier-general on 24 May and was ordered to hurry his 4th Armoured Division to the Abbeville front during the night of 26-27 May. He had recently been marked for the great northward attack across the Somme, but then that was cancelled. Then he was tapped for a drive against Amiens which in turn was shelved. Now he was to subdue the bridgehead the Germans had established based on the Monts de Caubert, high above Abbeville. The journey from the east had lost de Gaulle some 30 tanks, but on his arrival he found his force augmented by the French 19th and 47th Tank

Battalions and the 7th RDP, motorised Dragoons. In all he had 140 tanks in working order, although they were the usual mish-mash of marques, with all the repair and supply problems that implied. In addition he had, with the arrival of the 22nd Colonial Infantry Regiment and the 2nd Cavalry Division's artillery, six infantry battalions and six artillery groups. He arrived on Tuesday 28 May to find the 10th Army shaken by the previous day's failure to reduce the bridgehead and the Germans moving fresh troops of the XXXVIII Army Corps, 9th and 57th Infantry Divisions, into the sector. In conference at the Château d'Oisemont at noon on Tuesday de Gaulle decided to leave the British tanks in reserve and use his heavy armour against the German salient. The British 51st (Highland) Division was also to be in reserve as it, too, had just arrived from the Maginot Line and was unfamiliar with the terrain.

At 6 p.m. the attack went in. The more heavily-armoured Somuas and Chars B of the French were able to brush aside the German 3.7mm anti-tank fire in a way the thin-skinned British tanks could not. The

BELOW **An A 13 Mark II of the 10th Hussars knocked out at Huppy on 25 May.** (TM 1326/A2)

initial objectives were gained by nightfall, Huppy was once more in French hands and over 300 prisoners had been taken. At 4 a.m. the next morning the assault resumed, at first putting the shaken German defenders to flight. The battle lasted through the day and gave the French control of all the ground except the Monts de Caubert themselves and the lower hills alongside the Somme. The cost had been high and the Germans were reinforcing their positions during the hours of darkness. De Gaulle wrote:

'Only Mont Caubert still held out. There were a great many dead from both sides on the field. Our tanks had been sorely tried. Barely a hundred were still in working order. But all the same, an atmosphere of victory hovered over the battlefield. Everyone held his head high. The wounded were smiling. The guns fired gaily. Before us, in a pitched battle, the Germans had retired.'

The joy was short-lived. Although the French held against a German counter-attack the following day, their subsequent attempt to take the mount failed. In three days the 4th Armoured had lost over 100 tanks and 750 men killed in action. They could do no more.

On Tuesday 4 June the 10th Army tried again. The French 2nd Armoured Division, patched up after its mauling by Gruppe von Kleist, still had 17 Renault B1bis and was reinforced with a further three companies with these machines. With other units added to its strength, it had an on-paper complement of 50 Chars B, 35 Hotchkiss and 80 Renault Rs, but a couple of dozen of these were, in fact, unserviceable. Major-general Victor Fortune of the 51st (Highland) Division was in command of the armour, his own unit and the French 31st Infantry Division. The artillery opened up at 3.30 a.m. On the left the French infantry did poorly, confused and disorientated by friendly fire. The tanks ran into an undetected minefield and the advance petered out. Another minefield held up the tanks in the centre although some got through to face fire from the artillery and 88mm flak guns now defending the Monts de Caubert. The 152nd Brigade's 2nd Seaforth Highlanders were with the first wave and the 4th Seaforths with the second, neither making much progress and both suffering heavily. The Chars B were refuelled where they were, under fire from the Germans, but even this gallant act was not sufficient to keep them moving forward. To the right of the main road from Blangy to Abbeville the 4th Queen's Own Cameron Highlanders met concentrated machine-gun fire and could go no further. Further west, around Cambron, 2nd Lieutenant Barker of the 1st Gordon Highlanders, was preparing for action.

'On the 4th June at 3.30am we attacked the German bridgehead our objective being The Bois de Cambron. This was our first full-scale attack with plenty of artillery

ABOVE **Men of the 2nd Seaforth Highlanders prepare to defend their ground.**
(IWM F4626)

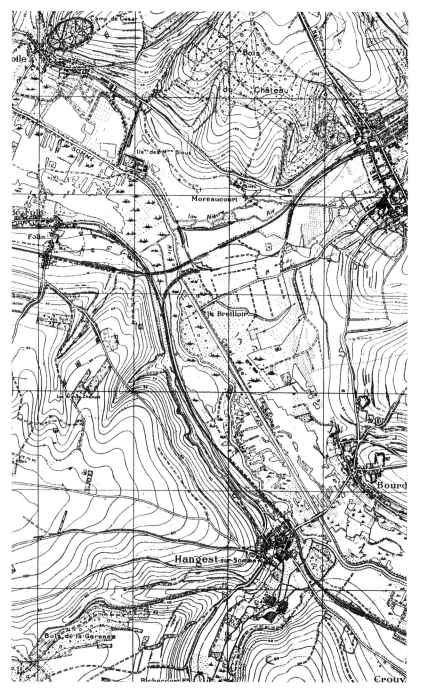

support; indeed it was probably the first set piece attack by the British Army in the 1939-45 war. There was a mixture of excitement in the air with apprehension lest we were found wanting as we prepared for the assault and had our evening meal.'

The 4th The Black Watch and 1st Gordon Highlanders went well, taking the ridge overlooking the river and getting down to the river itself at Gouy. But the commanding heights of the Monts de Caubert remained in German hands, making it impossible to hold the ground. Of the 73 tanks with which the French 2nd Armoured had started the day, 27 had been knocked out and six failed mechanically. Only six Chars B were still operational and another 28 AFVs were scarcely mobile. The attack was over.

ROMMEL ON THE SOMME

Army Group B opened Operation Red on Wednesday 5 June. Bridges over the Somme had been blown, but the plan to launch an attack against the southern flank of the panzers to meet a similar attack from the north had required certain bridges to be preserved, including those between Condé-Folie and Hangest-sur-Somme six miles (10km) north-west of Amiens railway crossings. The valley of the Somme is a marshy lowland in which the river splits up into numerous channels and is diverted to form lakes by the people who live there. On the southern flank the waterway presses up against abrupt hills while the slope to the north is less steep. On either side rolling country offers easy travelling to AFVs. To oppose the Germans between Amiens and the Channel coast was the French 10th Army, with the 51st (Highland) Division on the coast and the remains of the British 1st Armoured Division on the River Bresle which runs north-west to the sea at le Tréport. To their rear, holding a line on the Béthune river running south-east from Dieppe towards Forges-les-Eaux and then south to the Seine on the line of the Andelle river, was Beaumanforce. This was an ad hoc formation under Brigadier A. B. Beauman reporting to Lieutenant-general Sir Henry Karslake, the commander of the British lines of communication troops, who reported direct to General Georges. From General Georges

ABOVE **The bridges over the Canal de la Somme and the river itself were north-west of le Breilloir, north of Hangest. Only the more northerly of the two survives. There is a German cemetery at Bourdon.** (BL C21 (15) sheet XXII-8/3-4. WW2Maps/3/34)

OPPOSITE TOP **The bridge over the Somme Canal between Gouy and Petit Port, known to medieval historians as Blanchetaque. When this was a marsh, Edward III crossed here before Crecy and here Henry V attempted to cross and failed on his long route to Agincourt.** (MME Mon/Diep98/2/9)

OPPOSITE MIDDLE **The two bridges now stand on the banks of a lake. On the left, by the red car, the surviving railway line and, beyond the footbridge, the framework of an iron bridge marks the stump of the southern embankment.** (MME WW2/9/3)

OPPOSITE BOTTOM **From the D3 north-west of Hangest the barrier of the Somme can be appreciated. The track still runs along the slope and beyond the trees that now obscure the view to the right the railway can be seen.** (MME WW2/8/35)

communication flowed down to General Altmayer's 10th Army and through 10th Army channels to the 51st Division. A ready prescription for confusion. Between Abbeville and Amiens the French defenders were predominantly colonial troops, men of the same temper as those who had fought so well in the north.

On Wednesday 5 June Rommel went to see the artillery barrage designed to prevent the French getting near and blowing the bridges that took the railway over the water and the road near Condé-Folie.

'The preparatory barrage, which started punctual to the minute, made an extraordinarily impressive sight from our excellent vantage point. The flash of our shell-bursts seemed to be everywhere and there was little to be heard of enemy counter-fire... News reached us at about 05.00 hours that the railway and road bridges had fallen intact into our hands. Part of the Engineer Battalion was already hard at work on the railway bridge, unbolting rails and clearing away sleepers, in order to prepare the way for the division to cross with its vehicles.'

The opposition was light, only a handful of men of the 5th Colonial Infantry who had slogged up on foot over 18 miles (30km) the previous day. Nonetheless Rommel found himself having to take cover more than once under their fire. The crossing was delayed for a while when a tank shed a track on the narrow causeway, but by 9 a.m. the flow was restored. They were still under fire from Hangest to the south-east as noon approached and, as 5th Panzer had been held up after crossing at Pont-Remy, south-east of Abbeville, Rommel decided that had to be stopped and 7th Panzer should move on. It was a tougher assignment than he realised; Weygand's 'hedgehogs', strong-points, were showing their value.

Rommel reports:

'To eliminate the enemy force in Hangest ... a whole panzer battalion was launched against the western outskirts of the village... We watched the battalion approach closer and closer to the village and very soon heard their fire. Then the tanks turned off up the hill to the west, but only a few surmounted the topmost ridge. Most of them stuck on the hill... The crews, who dismounted from their tanks, were suddenly fired on by enemy machine-guns and suffered casualties in the coverless terrain.'

Self-propelled guns were brought up to bombard the village and the Motor-cycle Battalion ordered to attack and clear it on foot, which they did, though not before Rommel again found himself under machine-gun fire. The 5th Company of the 44th Colonial Infantry had given an outstanding account of themselves. It was not until 3 p.m. that Rommel was able to move out of the bridge-head and the building of a heavy-duty bridge at Hangest could not start that day.

At Quesnoy-sur-Airaines they ran into colonial infantry installed behind the walls of the château to the east of the village and endured heavy fire from them. The barrage from the panzers in response

ABOVE **An accident held up No. 2 Platoon, 3rd Company when PzKpfw IV No.321 lost a track. It had to be pushed down the bank, where it can be seen to the left of the bridge, to allow the column to pass. It was repaired and rejoined the Division in a matter of hours. The aircraft is a Henschl 126.** (IWM RML 193)

RIGHT **Once across the bridges, 7th Panzer had to climb the hills and deal with heavy fire from Hangest.** (IWM RML 252)

overcame the resistance and the tanks flowed round the village. At Airaines itself the resistance lasted three full days as the 53rd Colonial Infantry refused to give in. Reprisals followed, few prisoners were taken.

By evening 7th Panzer was just short of Montagne-le-Fayel, seven miles (11km) from the Somme. Rommel reports that strong attacks were made on his right flank by tanks and coloured troops that evening, but they were fought off. On Thursday 6 June they halted south of the Amiens-Rouen road, south-west of Poix-de-Picardie and on Friday

'The advance went straight across country, over roadless and trackless fields, uphill, downhill, through hedges, fences and high cornfields. The route taken by the tanks was so chosen that the less cross-country-worthy vehicles of the 37th Reconnaissance Battalion and the 6th Rifle Regiment could follow in their track-prints. We met no enemy troops, apart from a few stragglers …'

That day they reached Ménerval, close to the Forges-les-Eaux to Gournay-en-Bray road. The 51st Division, on the Bresle, had been comprehensively outflanked.

THE CLOSING TRAP

General Evans went to see his superior, General Altmayer, on that Friday 7 June. He proposed the use of the remaining tanks, 37 Mark VIs and 41 cruisers, for an attack against the panzers' flank decisively to halt their envelopment on the western half of the 10th Army. That evening General Weygand arrived at 10th Army headquarters and ordered Evans to scatter his tanks along the line of the River Andelle in support of the infantry. Evans protested that his force was entirely unsuitable for such a static task, but Weygand was adamant and the 1st Armoured was condemned to futile destruction.

The 2nd/6th Battalion East Surrey Regiment came under Beauforce on 18 May (Commander, Lieutenant-colonel Heseltine, DSC, MC) under 30 minutes notice to move, according to the abridged war diary prepared by Captain H. H. Walker. They had spent the previous fortnight working in the docks at Le Havre and had just received orders to depart for the Saar front when these new instructions were issued. They were an infantry pioneer battalion and had only four 2-inch mortars, but only one with sights, no 3-inch mortars and no mortar ammunition. There were only 11 anti-tank (Boyes) rifles and 16 Bren guns, but no tracer ammunition, no grenades, no revolvers, no compasses and no field glasses. Their transport was short by three 15-cwt trucks, a water cart, and an 8-cwt truck. Evidently there was an emergency. At 8 p.m. they were put on 15 minutes notice to move. At 10 p.m. the notice to move was cancelled and they were told to be ready at first light.

For the next two days the 2/6th East Surreys were on the River Bresle near Gamache, ten miles (16km) from the coast at Le Tréport, but were then withdrawn to Arques-la-Bataille on the river south of Dieppe. Their

patrols encountered probing patrols of Germans from time to time. Stanley Rayner, a despatch rider mounted on a Norton motor-cycle, was on one such patrol early on.

'A patrol consisted of one light 15-cwt truck with a driver and an officer in the cab, whilst on the back (which was open) was mounted a Bren gun – a light machine-gun – with also a Boyes Anti-Tank Rifle, supposedly capable of stopping any known tank. Hopefully this time we had the correct ammunition. Six motorcycle Despatch Riders completed these patrols, four in front and two behind.'

Rayner carried a short Lee Enfield with five rounds of ammunition. They drove across a peaceful countryside for some distance before coming on an improvised road-block made of farm machines which left a narrow space through which they could pass, at least the motorcycles could, for moments later the four leading riders found themselves alone. The trucks were still behind the road-block.

'The leading despatch riders stopped … We stayed put with our engines running. Now Mac could speak fluent French and coming towards him was a lady on foot who must have been French. The next minute 'all hell' broke loose. Bullets showered down the road at us like hailstones passing us as well as ricocheting off the roadstones… As for Mac and the lady, they had completely disappeared. I never saw the going of them at all.'

Rayner crawled back along the ditch to his patrol and the other despatch riders also made it back, one wounded. Of the lady there is no further report.

BELOW **The First World War memorial in Hangest bears a tribute to the civilian casualties of Rommel's assault.** (MME WW2/8/36)

RIGHT **German dead lie in the cemetery east of Bourdon, north-east of the river.** (MME WW2/8/32)

BELOW **The French colonial dead lie at Condé-Folie, north of Hangest.** (MME WW2/9/7)

LEFT **Panzer 38(t)s and Panzer IIs attack the French colonial troops' positions behind the château's circuit wall at Quesnoy-sur-Airaines.** (IWM RML 276)

BELOW **The breaches made in the wall by Rommel's tanks have now been bricked up.** (MME WW2/9/15)

The 2/6th East Surreys handed over to the 4th Sherwood Foresters and were withdrawn to Bihorel, near Rouen, on 31 May to become part of 1st Support Group, 1st Armoured Division. With 101st Light Anti-Aircraft and Anti-Tank Regiment's 44 2-pounder anti-tank guns, they were to defend the line between Aumale in the north and Forges-les-Eaux in the south. It was a distance of 20 miles (32km) on the ground, a density of about one gun every 800 yards (750m). The 4th Border Regiment would be on their left, north of Aumale, further down the stream that was the start of the River Bresle. The East Surreys took up positions along the road south of Aumale towards Abancourt, the guns overlooking the open country to the east. Tuesday 4 June was spent improving their defences. On Wednesday the bombing began. Aumale railway station was hit, but the Surreys' positions escaped notice. Lieutenant John Redfern was sent to establish contact with the Borders, but they were not there. They had been sent to hold the route back to Le Havre, but no one told the Surreys and no one took their place; the flank was open.

The bombing on Thursday 6 June was supported by machine-gun fire, and now the Germans seemed to know exactly where they were. It boded ill for the morrow. John Redfern was in a position on the hillside due south of Aumale and overlooking the hamlet of Fleuzy through which the railway ran. On Friday the French 12th Light Cavalry Regiment arrived and established themselves in Redfern's positions. It was then, at 3 p.m., that the Englishman learned that the Germans had already penetrated the Surreys' front to the south and taken Abancourt in the direction of which the French were attacking southwards along the railway. At about 5 p.m. two German lorries full of infantry came north, from Redfern's right, and were destroyed on the road by the 2-pounder anti-tank gun. Infantry on foot followed, took cover when the Surreys opened fire

and started trying to work round their flanks. The Bren guns stopped them and there was a stand-off until 7.30 p.m., neither side having the advantage. Then refugees appeared, making their way along the road from Aumale and up the hill to the south. Redfern wrote:

'They were stopped by the Germans in the orchard [to his front] and as they moved up the road so did the Germans move up behind them. They put the refugees on the sky-line with some of the troops they had already captured and moved all their forces round to my right flank. About ten minutes later some hand grenades were thrown at our defences one of which burst underneath the anti-tank gun, wounding very seriously the crew and disabling the gun. Firing then began on my right, left and rear. The enemy had apparently encircled our position. After five minutes exchange of fire and hand grenades I was called upon to surrender, this I refused to do. The

demand was twice repeated and again I refused so with a "Heil Hitler!" and shouting Hurrah they charged. Just before they charged I ordered the men to fix bayonets. The Germans charged to about five yards [4.5m], saw our bayonets and stopped.'

Although the Surreys fired on them as they came, the Germans had sub-machine guns which forced Redfern's men to take cover and firing and counter-firing continued for a while, when the Germans pulled back to loot the British truck. Further exchanges of fire took place as darkness came and at 10 p.m. Redfern was able to get out of his weapon-pit and assess the situation. Four other men were alive. They made off to the rear but ran into a German patrol. Redfern was wounded and let the others go on without him. They were captured, Redfern was found next morning by the 12th Light Cavalry and sent to hospital in the rear.

Those Surreys further south of Redfern received the unexpected reinforcement of a squadron of the 18th Dragon Portés. They were on the line of a track that still runs west from the Aumale-Abancourt road at the summit, half-sunken, as Captain Alex Thomson

OPPOSITE TOP **The memorial to Captain N'Tchorere near the church in Airaines.** (MME WW2/9/13)

OPPOSITE BOTTOM **Prisoners taken at Quesnoy-sur-Airaines are marched over the planked-over railway bridge across the Somme.** (IWM RML 280)

ABOVE **Aumale seen from a position a little to the north of Redfern's weapon pits.** (MME WW2/9/24)

LEFT **The valley of the Andelle and the road bridges at Normanville.** (MME WW2/9/32)

RIGHT **A somewhat distorted map, as comparison with a modern road map shows, of the fighting south and west of Aumale.** (QRSRM MME WW2/0/8)

BELOW **Detail from Sheet 4 of the German** *Strassenkarte von Nordostfrankreich*, **Berlin, 1940. Downstream, that is west, of Rouen there are no bridges, only ferries. Rommel attempted to take the bridges at Elbeuf, south of Rouen. The Andelle flows through Fleury, south-east of Rouen, to join the Seine at the Côte des Deux Amants. Les Andeleys is bottom right.**

(BL C21e1. MME WW2MF2/18)

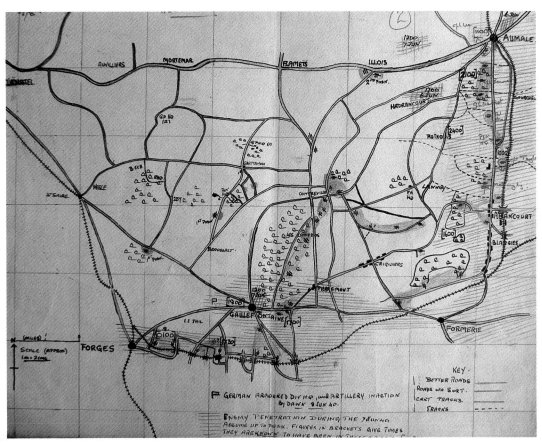

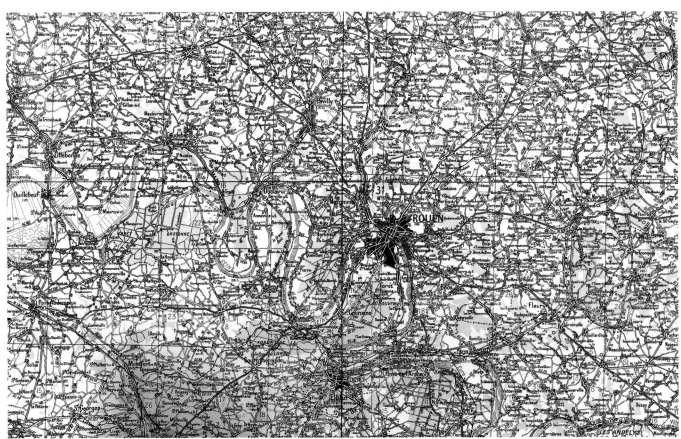

remarked, like a Sussex lane. Together they held against the Panzer Division, probably the 5th and not Rommel's 7th as folklore has it, well on into Saturday, when, before they could be surrounded, they withdrew. The only officer remaining unwounded in this group, 2nd Lieutenant John Naylor, brought 21 men back to Battalion headquarters.

Rommel was hurrying forwards further south, over the wide plains that separate the valley of the Somme from that of the Seine. He was approaching the defensive positions along the River Andelle. To call it a river is to accord it greater respect than the reality deserves; it is a large stream rather than even a small river. As a moat against an enemy it is trivial here. The bridge at Sigy, five miles (8km) south-west of Forges-les-Eaux, was blown by C Brigade of what was now Beauman Division on the morning of Saturday 8 June, just as 7th Panzer attacked. Rommel saw what was happening and while the defenders were engaged by the howitzer battery,

'... I reconnoitred the chances of getting tanks across the river and found a point 400 yards [365m] south of Sigy where it could be forded ... Although there was over three feet [1m] of water near the eastern bank, the first tanks crossed without any trouble ... However, when the first Panzer II attempted it, its engine cut out in midstream, leaving the crossing barred to all other vehicles. Meanwhile several British soldiers had waded across to us with hands up, and, with their help, our motor-cyclists started to improve the crossing.'

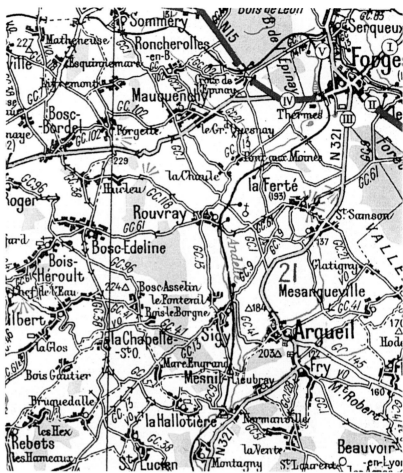

They cut down willows and plundered the ruins of a railway bridge to improve the crossing and a Panzer III came back to pull the obstructive tank out of the water. Just then Rommel learned that one of his reconnaissance troops had found the bridges intact at Normanville and had prevented their being blown. The effort was diverted to the immediate south and Sigy was finally taken from the west at 2 p.m. with the capture of some 100 British.

Then began a gallop for the Seine. At 8 p.m. a company of the Panzer Regiment was sent to block any counter-attack from Rouen while Rommel himself intended to seize the bridges over the Seine at Elbeuf later that day. His forces kept running into small groups of British or French attempting to withdraw southwards. As darkness fell word came that the western flank was secure and off Rommel went along the ridge around which the Seine swings in a huge meander south of Rouen.

'We had great difficulty in the darkness and with our inadequate maps in following the route. The noise of our passage as we drove through the villages wakened people from their sleep, and brought them rushing out into the street to welcome us – as British... We turned south at Les Athieux and reached the village of Sotteville at midnight – the first German troops to reach the Seine.'

ABOVE **The Andelle valley runs south from Forges-les-Eaux. Sigy is due west of, and Normanville south-west of, Argueil. From** *Strassenkarte von Nordostfrankreich, Blatt 4,* **Berlin 1940.** (BL C21e1. MME WW2Maps/3/27)

LEFT **The Andelle and the new bridge at Sigy-en-Bray.** (MME WW2/9/26)

ABOVE **From the Côte des Deux Amants looking due west towards Elbeuf, the ridge around which this great meander of the Seine is formed can be seen to the right.** (MME WW2/10/24)

They turned west along the riverside and into the outskirts of Elbeuf. The motor-cycle Battalion was sent ahead to take the bridges and keep them open. At 1.30 a.m. on Sunday 9 June Rommel himself went forward to see what was happening. His men were snarled up in traffic jams in the town. Civilians were hurrying through the streets and over the bridges. Rommel's troops were close to the bridges but still hesitated to go for them. They were ordered to attack at once and at 3 a.m. did so. They were too late. The bridges went up as soon as they advanced. The opportunity, to Rommel's fury, was lost.

North of Rouen, at Isneauville, Saturday was a bad day for the advancing 5th Panzer. Lieutenant-colonel A. G. Syme of the Royal Scots was in command of another scratch unit, four companies of infantry, a platoon of machine-guns and four anti-tank guns. Beauman ordered him to hold the road north of Rouen, and this he did for a full day. A German tank obligingly stranded itself in the middle of the road when it tried to rush their wire and found it mined. It was not until 7 p.m. that Syme's position was threatened with a flanking movement, and he then withdrew to his second line of defence and continued to hold his enemies at bay. At dusk the Germans pulled back and Syme's force slipped away south of the Seine, leaving 12 knocked-out tanks to show there was a sting in the tail of the BEF. The 5th Panzer Division entered Rouen, the lowest point at which the river was bridged at that time, the next day. The bridges had been destroyed. The remains of the French 10th Army, the 51st Division with them, could now only leave by sea.

ANOTHER BEACH

The German advance of Wednesday 5 June at the seaward end of the Somme line had overwhelmed the men of the 51st Division in the front line, determinedly though they fought. The 7th and 8th Argyll and Sutherland Highlanders had much too wide a front to hold and suffered accordingly. The 1st Gordons got out of Gouy, near the river, and where Edward III had crossed on the way to Crécy, the Germans now crossed in the opposite direction. By the end of the day the 51st were on the line of the Bresle in the west and a little forward of it in the east. Fortune requested permission to pull back to the river but Altmayer, bound by Weygand's orders, refused. Indeed, Weygand was swift to accuse the British of preparing to run for home. They were, in any case, forced to retire across the Bresle at Blangny as darkness fell on Thursday 6 June, the Lothian & Border Yeomanry having endured relentless attacks at Oisemont all day in the company of a troop of bloody-minded and aggressive Frenchmen in armoured cars.

Lieutenant-general James Marshall-Cornwall had been sent to France as Head of No. 17 Military Mission a week before with instructions to attach himself to the headquarters of the 10th Army. He now cabled London to give the news that Altmayer was unable, because of technical breakdown, to communicate with either superiors or subordinates and what was more, to give his opinion that the General had himself broken down and was incapable of command. Marshall-Cornwall entreated Altmayer to give orders for IX Corps, including the 51st, to fall

back on the River Béthune, but he would not. Meanwhile 5th and 7th Panzer were forging south. On Saturday 8 June General Ihler, commanding IX Corps, received Weygand's order to fall back in the direction of Rouen-Les Andelys, the area Rommel was driving through later that day. It would take four days as the French had to slog it on foot and their artillery was horse-drawn. The 51st, thoroughly motorised, could have done the trip in a day, but elected, in the words of General Fortune, to fight their way back with them step by step. By Saturday evening they were outside Dieppe and the next day news came that they were cut off from Rouen. Le Havre had to be the objective. Ihler agreed.

Fortune immediately set up Arkforce at Arques-la-Bataille under Brigadier A. C. L. Stanley-Clarke to hurry west to establish an enclave at the end of the Le Havre peninsula. He had 1st Black Watch and the surviving men of 7th and 8th Argyll & Sutherland Highlanders as well as artillery and machine-gun units. On Monday 10 June Admiral Sir William James, C-in-C Portsmouth, arrived in Le Havre and decided to move the small craft to St Valery-en-Caux to improve the chances of getting the men off. That day Rommel was moving once more, this time towards the sea to cut off retreat. They were in sight of Yvetot by 10.30 a.m.

'As we approached the main Cany-Fécamp road [south-east of St Valery] a despatch rider from the

Reconnaissance Battalion reported that Captain von Luck had found enemy lorry columns on the main road and was rounding them up… It had every appearance of being a considerable formation… A quick interrogation revealed that it was the beginning of 31st French Division, which was to have embarked at Fécamp that afternoon… With my signals section I drove on in advance of the regiment through Les Petites Dalles and down to the water.'

Rommel was nine miles (15km) west of St Valery-

en-Caux. The Allies were surrounded.

The 2nd/6th East Surreys were fighting and falling back to fight again against 5th Panzer. Stanley Rayner, like most others, was thoroughly confused. His second Norton cycle had been lost and, on Sunday 10 June, he was riding in a truck.

'I knew not anymore where we were heading, for between the many French soldiers blocking our way and the German forces, we went hither and thither… Each stop we had to make, especially at night, we assumed

ABOVE **Graves of the 51st (Highland) Division at Franleu, west of Abbeville.** (MME Mon/Diep98/1/34)

RIGHT **In the Canadian CWGC Cemetery in Dieppe, devoted mainly to the fallen of the Dieppe Raid of 19 August 1942, some of the men and women killed in 1940 are buried.** (MME Mon/Diep98/3/25)

Carrier that had been hi[t]
alight with bullets expl[o]
ducked down, going on ta[...]
tower of a large house, loo[k]
along… We had made [...]
corner, so to speak.'

The town was crow[ded]
full of ships, more than [...]
radio and all blinded by [...]
destroyer covering the o[...]
further east, to Veules[...]
down from the high gr[ound]
course of what is said to [...]
past the holiday homes [...]
the narrow beach. A mix[...]
British boats took them [...]
and 900 French troops [...]
Valery, very few. The t[...]
and a number of Dut[ch]
beach to the west of the [...]
and started loading. Th[...]
soon saw what was happ[...]
with the flames of bur[...]
badly shot up and only a[...]
to Newhaven. As W[...]
Rommel was confident [...]
control. The troops s[...]
established in depth, rea[...]

LEFT **Panzer IV No. B01 of 2nd Battalion, 25th Panzer Regiment, manoeuvres onto the beach at Petites Dalles, 10 June.** (IWM RML 318)

BELOW **A sketch map of the 2nd/6th East Surreys' position at Beaunay (spelled Beaumais in error). North is at the foot of the sketch.** (QRSRM MME WW2/0/6)

defence positions. Patrols went out, staff cars and motor cycles to ascertain availability of roads. Many never returned… Chaotic is a possible word for the situation. However, we eventually arrived at a place called Beauney. [Beaunay, just over 4 miles (7km) north of Tôtes.] We turned into the grounds of Beauney, a Château in a wooded area with a huge green field in front of it and a road, tree lined, around it.'

The transport pulled in like a wild west wagon circle and they took up defensive positions. No sooner had they settled in than, at about 6 p.m., they came under fire. Rumour had it that Fifth Columnists were the problem, but it soon became apparent that they were under German attack.

'Two of my cousins in the East Surrey TA who were drivers in the Transport went down, under fire, and drove some of our trucks out to the Château end. We were ordered into the trucks ready to move on when our Despatch Rider, Ted Riley, got shot… Words failed me for he was so quietly confident. He would be missed …'

The attack was driven off by 7.30 and they were soon back on the road. Not long after they were fired on again. The transport was abandoned and, in small parties, they continued on foot.

On Tuesday 11 June the forces constituting IX Corps, the French 2nd and 5th Light Cavalry, 31st and 40th Infantry and the 51st (Highland) Division, had formed a defensive perimeter around St Valery-en-Caux from le Tot on the coast to the west and inland through Ingouville, Neville, le Mesnil-Durdent, Houdetot, St-Pierre-le-Vigier and Veules-les-Roses, with the Highlanders on the flanks and the French

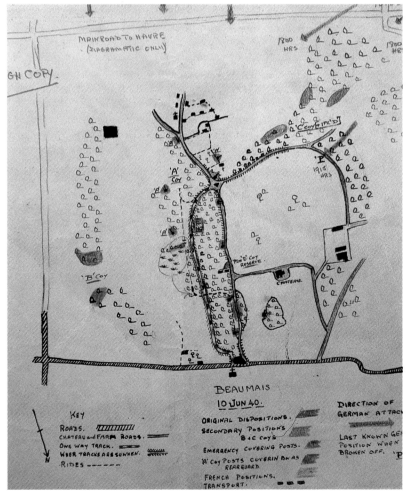

MAIN ROAD TO HAVRE
(DIAGRAMATIC ONLY)

BEAUMAIS
10 JUN 40.

KEY

ROADS.
CHATEAU & FARM ROADS.
ONE WAY TRACK.
WHER TRACKS ARE SUNKEN.
RIDES

ORIGINAL DISPOSITIONS.
SECONDARY POSITIONS
B & C COYS
EMERGENCY COVERING POSTS.
'A' COY POSTS COVERING B & C'S
REARGUARD
FRENCH POSITIONS.
TRANSPORT.

DIRECTION OF
GERMAN ATTACK

LAST KNOWN GE[R]
POSITION WHEN
BROKEN OFF.

RIGHT **The memorial to the French 2nd Cavalry Division stands to the west of St Valery-en-Caux, facing the obelisk of the 51st (Highland) Division's monument on the opposite headland.** (MME Mon/Diep98/3/2)

BELOW **The Highland Division's memorial stands alongside a later German bunker. A swastika was drawn in the wet cement and dated Sept. 1943.** (MME Mon/Diep98/3/5)

ABOVE **French and Bri
troops surrender on t
ground west of St Val
Caux.** (IWM RML 400)

BELOW **The watermills
border the path down
sea at Veules-les-Ro**
(MME Mon/Diep98/3/7)

lying about everywhere … While the tanks were moving round the southern side of the harbour towards the eastern quarter of the town, I followed the infantry across the narrow bridge to the market square. The town hall and many buildings round it were either already burnt out or still burning… A few minutes later the French General Ihler came up to me wearing an ordinary plain military overcoat… The General declared himself ready to accept my demand for the immediate capitulation of his force.'

General Fortune, unaware of this meeting and still hopeful of evacuation that evening, sent a message to Ihler saying the 51st would fight on no matter what the French elected to do. The reply came back that a cease-fire would begin at 8 a.m. There was no choice but to comply.

Stanley Rayner woke to the new day.

'What we could see … the next morning … having slept on top of a real bed for the heck of a long time, was a lot of badly battered buildings bombed and strafed. They looked to have had a pretty rough time of it. The date was June 12th, one that was to live in my memory for a long time.

'It seemed to have gone unusually quiet. Our Sgt having gone down to see what was happening, we were just milling about… The Sgt came back. It must have been about 10.30 a.m. He said we had to "surrender", and must destroy our weapons and equipment. We had very little. However, I still had my five rounds of ammunition. It was difficult to use a rifle riding a motor cycle as a Despatch Rider. To say that I was shaken by

having to surrender was mild. This was not possible. My feeling was indescribable. It was demoralising. I was shattered, despondent and deflated in turn… What would my Dad, the old soldier, be thinking?'

In Le Havre the men of Arkforce were shipping out, leaving wrecked transport and equipment behind them. The Germans now turned to cross the Seine.

ABOVE **French and British fallen lie side by side at St Valery-en-Caux.** (MME Mon/Diep98/2/3)

LEFT **General Ihler, in the képi, with Rommel left and, on the extreme right, General Fortune, by the harbour at St Valery-en-Caux.** (IWM RML 345)

THE FALL OF FRANCE

ABOVE **A private memorial to Leutnant Jürgen Hoesch and Obergefreiter Robert Preis stands by the D167 Boives-Sains road, south of Amiens, where their Panzer IV was destroyed on 5 June.** (MME WW2/10/4)

RIGHT **An isolated memorial to French resistance at Fleury, east of Poix-de-Picardie.** (MME WW2/8/20)

While Rommel was crossing the Somme, Army Group A and Panzer Gruppe Guderian were gathering themselves for their attack further east scheduled for Sunday 9 June. On the right, the west, of this front Army Group B's Gruppe von Kleist with two corps were to thrust forward from Amiens and Péronne on Wednesday 5 June, the same day as Rommel attacked the lower Somme front.

The French had adopted the strong-point strategy ordered by Weygand. As a method of disrupting and slowing the German advance it worked well, but the armoured, mobile strength to hit back once the disruption had been achieved was lacking. Kleist's men broke through relatively easily, but then had to subdue village after village. Their advance on this day was limited to some six to ten miles (10-15km) but the problem was solved by the success of 7th and 5th Panzers to the west who drove a great flanking cut into the Allied defences and by the advance to Soissons of the German 6th Army. The collapse of the front before Paris was swift. By Monday 10 June the Germans were across the Seine at Les Andelys and on the Marne at Château Thierry. That evening the French radio broadcast the news that the Government was leaving Paris. It moved to Tours and thence to Bordeaux.

THE TOUGH NUT

Rethel stands on the River Aisne some 25 miles (40km) north-east of Reims. The Canal des Ardennes runs alongside the river and the valley of the Aisne presented as much of an obstacle as it had in the previous war. For the 40 miles (65km) that separates Rethel from Châlons-sur-Marne the country is open, almost heathland, offering immense scope to mobile armour, if once the moat of the Aisne were overcome. The front to be attacked was between Château-Porcien in the west and Attigny in the east with Rethel in the centre. Eight crossing points were to be taken and Guderian thus released to seize the Plateau de Langres. Guderian was not keen on letting others take the crossings but Colonel-general Wilhelm List, commanding 12th Army, was not willing to put the panzers at unnecessary risk.

On Sunday 9 June the operation began. In the centre the German XXIII Corps was up against the 14th Infantry Division of General Jean de Lattre de Tassigny. General Albrecht Schubert had to allow that they fought in a manner reminiscent of the best

French troops at Verdun. To the east the 26th Infantry similarly held firm. Only in two places, on either side of Château-Porcien, had crossings been seized and a small bridge-head been made. Guderian proposed that the entire Panzer Group be moved there by night to cross the next day. The attack went ahead at 6.30 a.m. on Monday 10 June and made swift progress. Guderian wrote:

'Once in the open the tanks met hardly any resistance, since the new French tactics concentrated on the defence of woods and villages, while the open ground was abandoned out of respect for our tanks. Consequently our infantry had to fight hard for the barricaded streets and houses of the villages, while then tanks, only slightly inconvenienced by the French artillery firing to the rear from positions they still held on the Rethel front, broke straight through to the [river] Retourne and crossed that swampy stream, which had been dammed, at Neuflize. [Some seven miles (12km) south of Rethel.]'

They then turned east with 1st Panzer south of the river and Balck's Rifle Regiment north of it.

The power required to carry out the Weygand tactics was present on this front, in the shape of the 2nd Armoured Group or Groupement Buisson. It was made up mainly of the French 3rd Armoured Division, which had fought so determinedly at Stonne, and was still a force to be reckoned with. The three operational battalions had between them some

ABOVE **German troops clean up after the capture of St Sauflieu, seven miles (11km) south of Amiens, 7 June.**
(B95/60/9)

LEFT **Tank country; 1st Panzer Regiment, Gruppe Guderian, advances, 9 June 1940.**
(B80/32/30A)

RIGHT **Detail from the**
Gewässerabschnitte Nordost-
***Frankreich* map of February**
1940. The main roads
converge on Rethel at the
foot of square 23 and south
of the river and canal lies
open country.
(MME WW2Maps/2/12)

BELOW **The Renault B1 bis of**
Lieutenant Robert Godinat,
***Chambertin*, passing through**
Cauroy on its way to attack
Guderian's force at Juniville.
(TM 4995/E/6)

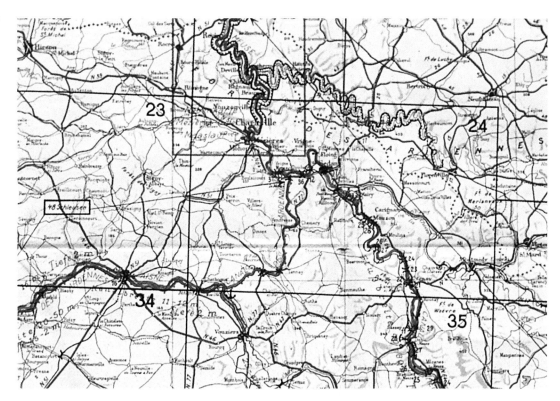

30 Chars B, 50 Hotchkiss H-39s and 40 Renault R-35s. Also available here was the 7th Light Mechanised Division a hastily-formed unit comprising troops who had survived the actions in Belgium and evacuation from Dunkirk. They could contribute 20 Hotchkiss H-35s in worn state and the same number of new Hotchkiss H-39s, as well as a couple of dozen armoured cars. In the afternoon the 7th Light Mechanised punched into 1st Panzer and got as far as Ménil-Lépinois while north of the river 3rd Armoured went for Perthes to help 127th Infantry withdraw. Guderian wrote of the day's events:

'Juniville was reached in the early afternoon, where the enemy counter-attacked with strong armoured forces. A tank battle developed to the south of Juniville, which lasted for some two hours before being eventually decided in our favour. In the course of the afternoon Juniville itself was taken. There Balck managed personally to capture the colours of a French regiment. The enemy withdrew to La Neuville [south of Juniville]. While the tank battle was in progress I attempted, in vain, to destroy a Char B with a captured 47mm anti-tank gun; all the shells I fired at it simply bounced harmlessly off its thick armour. Our 37mm and 20mm guns were equally ineffective against this adversary… In the late afternoon another heavy engagement with enemy tanks took place, this time to the north of Juniville… but we managed to beat them off.'

That evening General Buisson was ordered to pull his armoured group back and it was disbanded. The two halves were sent off to different armies, each depleted by the day's not unsuccessful efforts and now condemned to soldier on alone. The larger scene was depressing for the French. The Germans were now outflanking this theatre on the west and General Huntzinger ordered a withdrawal to a line from Reims to the end of the Maginot line at Montmédy. As for Guderian, he was exhausted. On returning to his group headquarters he cast himself down on a bale of straw and fell asleep. His adjutant, Lieutenant-colonel Riebel, had a tent erected over him and a guard posted to ensure his undisturbed sleep.

On Tuesday 11 June the drive south continued with 1st Panzer taking La Neuville and pushing on for Béthéniville, a village that was, Guderian remarks,

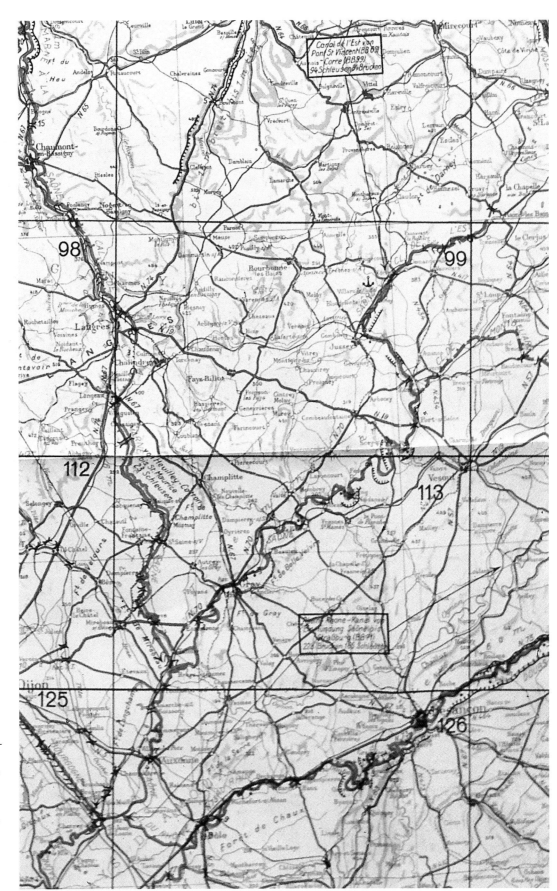

RIGHT **Detail from the
*Gewässerabschnitte Nordost-
Frankreich* map of February
1940. Langres is on the
Marne/Saône Canal in square
98 and Gray in 113. Belfort
lies some 37 miles (60km)
east of Vesoul, top right in
square 113.** (MME WW2Maps/2/31)

familiar to him from the previous war. There, on the little River Suippes, the French attacked again, the 7th Light Mechanised's Hotchkisses acting by themselves and failing to slow German progress. On Wednesday the Germans reached Châlons-sur-Marne and so keen were they to advance that infantry and tankmen were almost falling over each other to press forward. The French were riven in two. Order and counter-order from above sent the Gruppe Guderian swinging left and right, but he kept one of his corps firmly on the route south. On the afternoon of Thursday 13 June 1st Panzer reached the Rhine-Marne canal at Etrepy, between Vitry-le-François and Bar-le-Duc where General Rudolf Schmidt of XXXIX Corps ordered Balck to stop to let the rest close up. When Guderian arrived he found Balck curiously coy about his positions and reluctant to admit to having crossed the canal and established a bridgehead. On discovering that Balck had disobeyed orders in creeping forward Guderian countermanded the order and reiterated his firm policy of pressing on as fast as possible. They reached St Dizier during the night.

Friday 14 June saw the Germans enter the open city of Paris, armed with cameras and behaving like tourists. Guderian was still on his travels.

'At midday … I entered St Dizier. The first person I saw was my friend, Balck, seated on a chair in the market-place. He was looking forward to a few quiet hours after all the effort of the last few days and nights. I had to disappoint him in this… Balck was ordered to set off at once and to head straight for Langres.'

He got there, over 50 miles (85km) further south,

that night and took the surrender of the garrison of the fortress on Saturday morning, with 3,000 prisoners. The pace did not slacken. By the evening 1st Panzer was at Gray-sur-Saône, another 30 miles (50km) south-east. By Monday 17 June, Guderian's birthday, 29th (Motorised) Infantry Division was on the Swiss border. It had taken them just over a week. The Maginot Line was now surrounded.

Orders were now given for Gruppe Guderian to swing east and north, which he was, in fact, already doing. In the morning of Tuesday 18 June he was in Belfort, the town which had stood against the Prussian invasion of 1870. Here the forts were still holding out. Guderian records:

'The division organised an assault group for the attack on the forts and on the citadel. The battle began about noon. The first fort to be captured was Basse-Perches, followed by Hautes-Perches, near where I was standing, and the citadel itself. The tactics employed were extremely simple: first, a short bombardment by the artillery of 1st Panzer Division; then Eckinger's rifle battalion, in armoured troop-carrying vehicles, and an 88mm anti-aircraft gun drove right up to the fort, the latter taking up position immediately in front of the gorge; the riflemen thus reached the glacis [slope under the wall] without suffering any casualties, climbed up it, clambered over the entrenchments and scaled the wall while the 88mm fired into the gorge at point-blank range. The fort was then summoned to surrender, which under the impact of the rapid attack it did…Our casualties were very light.'

BEYOND THE SEINE

The departure of the BEF from Dunkirk and the capture of the 51st (Highland) Division at St Valery were not the end of British presence in France, nor did it spell the disappearance of organised units. There had been, of course, a number of small parties making their way south over the Seine. John Naylor of the 2/6th East Surreys had taken the survivors of the men who, with the French, had opposed the German advance at Aumale in search of battalion headquarters. He recalled:

'… having no map or compass, finding it [H.Q.] was difficult. We proceeded in a westerly direction for some distance. We were very tired and hungry and at a farmhouse found enough eggs to give us one each. We ate them raw and I have never liked raw eggs since!

'… Shortly afterwards, as we were half-way across an open field, we heard and saw 15 or 20 German tanks crossing our front. We hit the ground smartly and, fortunately, they did not see us … As it grew darker we halted for the night. At dawn I decided it was unlikely we could find Battalion HQ and that it would be best to make for the river Seine, the next defensive line to the south … During the day we met other British troops withdrawing to the river Seine and arrived at a wood near the river to the east of Rouen that evening … The following morning [Saturday 8 June] we crossed the river by a bridge. There was a great deal of confusion, many rumours, and no sign of a defensive position being prepared along the river. I learnt that British troops were being collected at Le Mans and we made our way there

through Alençon: sometimes by truck, sometimes on foot … Of the 3 officers and 96 men of A Company … only I and 20 men returned.'

More organised was the arrival of 2/6th The Duke of Wellington's Regiment and 2/4th King's Own Yorkshire Light Infantry. They had been withdrawn from the Abbeville sector and sent to Rennes where they had been loading and unloading trains. On Friday 7 June they were back at Louviers, 15 miles (24km) south of Rouen on the southern bank of the Seine, as part of a group under the command of

ABOVE **At Le Quitteur, where the Saône is bridged just north of Gray, a mobile 15 cm. gun on a Panzer I chassis passes through the village.** (B84/68/15A)

LEFT **Crossing the Saône, 4.30 p.m., 15 June.** (B99/44/15)

General Duffour. The KOYLI were sent to hold the crossing at Pont de l'Arche and got embroiled with the flank guard of Rommel's failed attempt to get the bridge at Elbeuf. Fortunately the withdrawing French had omitted to take two anti-tank guns and their crews and these prevented the German armour crossing the bridge. Five companies of Yorkshiremen were cut off north of the river when the bridges were blown, but gave good account of themselves before managing to get back, swimming, in borrowed boats and some making use of a footbridge over a weir. Their losses amounted to only ten dead and 23 missing by the time all the stragglers had come back.

The 2/6th Dukes were upstream, guarding crossings at St Pierre-de-Vauvray, immediately east of Louviers, and at Les Andelys, overlooked by Richard Lion-Heart's Château Gaillard and the high cliffs that dominate the northern bank of the Seine as it swings through the repeated meanders as it passes Rouen. On Sunday 9 June they were joined by a couple of machine-gun units from 2nd Armoured Brigade and a single light tank. As French infantry started to arrive at about 11 a.m. the Germans appeared north of the river and the bridge at Les Andelys was blown. Mortar- and shell-fire poured down, followed by a dive-bomber attack. They were forced back first to Bernières and then to the neck of the meander at Venables. At the same time the British positions at St Pierre were assaulted and eventually out-flanked. The long line created by the winding river was beyond the powers of a single battalion to defend and German troops spilled over the Seine. With nightfall the pressure ceased, only to begin again on Monday 10 June. The Duke's commanding officer, Lieutenant-colonel Llewellyn, managed to find a senior officer to whom he could explain his men's predicament. Brigadier R. L. McCreery was in command of 2nd Armoured Brigade and was looking for his machine-gunners. He immediately promised to do what he could and was as good as his word. A small group of tanks arrived soon after and the German advance was checked. Their flanks, however, were now in the air and they were ordered back to the river Eure that evening.

It was at this stage, on 10 June, that Benito Mussolini decided that the Germans were going to win and that Italy had better join in to secure a place at the negotiating table. His troops attacked the French Alpine formations and were robustly and thoroughly thrown back.

General Sir John Dill, who became Chief of the Imperial General Staff in succession to Ironside in May, had sent for Lieutenant-general Alan Brooke immediately after his return from Dunkirk. He ordered Brooke to return to France and, under the title of II Corps, rebuild the BEF. In addition to the forces already over the Channel, Brooke would have the

52nd (Lowland) Division which was due to embark on 7 June and 1st Canadian Division which was then in Northamptonshire as a reserve to resist German forces invading East Anglia. There were no other troops to send. Brooke was not pleased. He regarded the whole exercise as futile now, except for some possible political usefulness. Reluctantly he went, arriving in Cherbourg on Wednesday 12 June, the day a large part of his command, the 51st, went into captivity.

Brooke met Weygand on Friday 14 June. Weygand confirmed that, as part of 3rd Army Group, the British

ABOVE **Advance of the group Koppenburg. Near Belfort, 19 June.** (B146/80/134/1)

LEFT **A 105mm howitzer is brought into action at Belfort, 4 p.m., 19 June.** (B80/134/0)

were to fall back on Rennes with a view to creating a redoubt in Brittany, an idea which Weygand himself pronounced impractical. Brooke accepted the order but immediately contacted London to say that he considered the position hopeless and that no more troops should be sent. Sensing reluctance to accept his view, Brooke telephoned Churchill himself and found his advocacy successful. He was released from French command and ordered to bring out everything he could.

South of the Seine a gap had opened between the French 10th Army, to which the British were attached, and the Army of Paris. The French 3rd Light Cavalry Division did what it could, but was unable to bridge the widening breach. Through it the infantry divisions of Army Group B poured towards the Loire.

Now the long quiescent Army Group C was released from its enforced lethargy in front of the Maginot Line. On Friday 14 June, with the French

ABOVE **The Château Gaillard, dominating the Seine at Les Andelys.** (MME WW2/10/31)

LEFT **The bitterness of defeat. French prisoners at Belfort, 23 June.** (B79/89/31)

LEFT **The cathedral rises miraculously above the ruins of Rouen.** (B126/335/30)

TOP RIGHT **Range-finding from the keep of the Château Gaillard.** (B126/340/31A)

CENTRE RIGHT **Refugees seek safety beyond the Loire – Gien, 19 June.** (B73/83/1)

BOTTOM RIGHT **The Germans push on through Normandy. Panzer 38(t)s on the road.** (IWM RML 436)

already starting to pull back their interval troops as part of their attempt to establish a line in touch with their forces to the west, the attack began. With their backs to the wall many of the French fought bitterly, but in four days' time the last of the fortifications had surrendered.

THE LAST DAYS

De Gaulle, now Under-Secretary for Defence in the French government, was in London early on Sunday 16 June to make arrangements for the evacuation of his government colleagues to North Africa, for Prime Minister Reynaud had expressed his determination not to give in. As he was washing in his room at the Hyde Park Hotel the French Ambassador, Pierre Corbin, and Jean Monnet, a member of the French Economic Mission, called on him. They informed de Gaulle that the request of France to be released from the undertaking not to enter into a separate peace was under consideration and also that they had worked out a plan with Sir Robert Vansittart, Under-Secretary at the Foreign Office, for, as de Gaulle, reports it,

"'... a plan which does seem striking. It would consist of a proposal for the union of France and England ... In the face of such a proposal, made in such circumstances, it is possible that Ministers may wish to think again and, at least, postpone surrender..." It was clear to me at once that the grandeur of the thing in any case made its rapid realisation impossible... But ... I consented ... to do what I could with Mr Churchill to get him to adopt it.'

As the day went on in a whirl of practical arrangements, de Gaulle was aware of the constant, unspoken question – what was to become of the French fleet? If France continued at war, as de Gaulle intended, the question would not arise. After a Cabinet meeting that evening Churchill told de Gaulle that the offer of union was approved. At 9.30 p.m. de Gaulle was back in Bordeaux. He discovered that Reynaud had resigned and that Marshal Pétain had been invited to form a government. Capitulation was now inevitable. On the morning of Monday 17 June, under the pretext of bidding farewell to General Sir Edward Spears who had been attached to the French government, Charles de Gaulle was back at the airport where the aircraft which had brought him home was, by arrangement, still waiting. He hopped in, accepting exile and the leadership of the Free French rather than surrender.

At 8 a.m. on Thursday 13 June, once the French had permitted him to come ashore, Sir Alan Brooke, as he now was, had set off for Le Mans where the Lines of Communication troops had their headquarters and which was the only remaining British establishment. He found that Generals Karslake and de Fonblanque had done little or nothing to reduce the number of non-combatant troops, the 'useless mouths', or repatriate the vast stores of ammunition and other

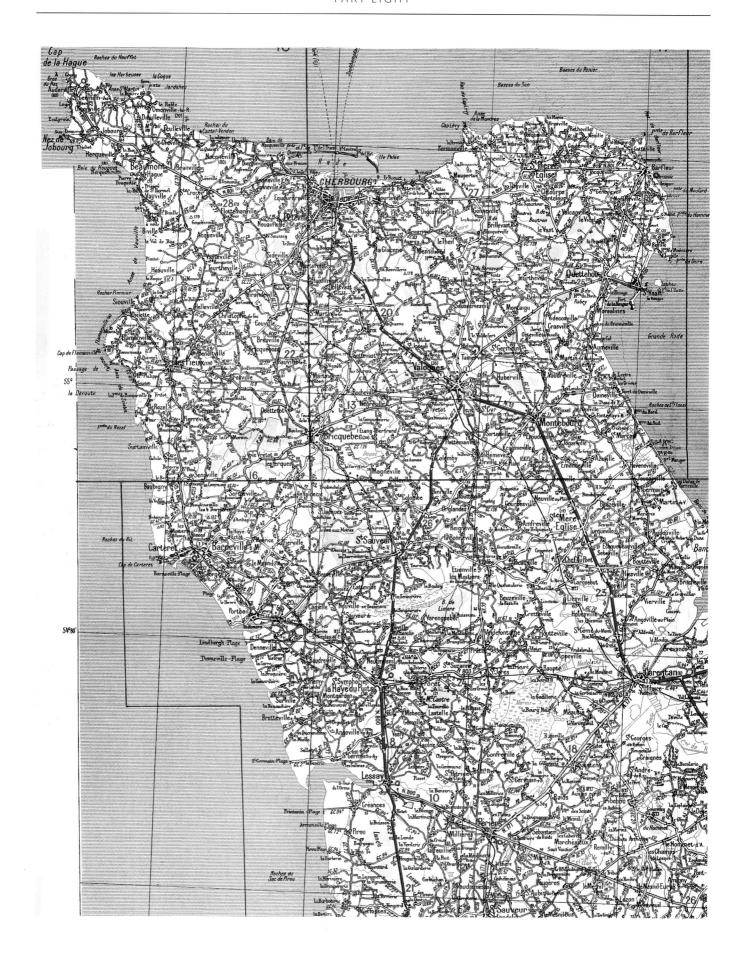

supplies that had been shipped to France in the last nine months. Indeed, the War Office was still behaving as if the object of the exercise was to increase British presence in France, sending people out to set up new depots. Now that he was released from French command, Brooke sent the Canadians back to Brest to re-embark, the 52nd Division to Cherbourg leaving a rearguard at the foot of the Cotentin peninsula to cover their retreat and the non-combatant parts of the Armoured Division to Nantes. That left some 7,000 Lines of Communication troops at Le Mans, 65,000 at Nantes and 20,000 at Rennes to be sent to appropriate embarkation points.

Then followed the difficult task of disentangling the British from the French without breaching the instruction to co-operate with them. Fortunately General Altmayer accepted gracefully that a parting of the ways had come. By the middle of Monday 17 June the British were moving up the Cotentin peninsula, 157th Brigade at Avranches and 3rd Armoured Brigade at St Lô. Lieutenant-general Marshall-Cornwell, whom Brooke had put in command of the troops formerly part of Altmayer's 10th Army, moved into Cherbourg to liaise with the French commander. It was Admiral Abrial, former commander at Dunkirk, once more presiding over a British departure. A defence line was set up through La Haye-du-Puits and

Germans would see again when Rommel was responsible for its defence in 1944, and on which much American blood would be spilled.

Rommel's 7th Panzer was ordered forward once more that same Monday with orders to go for Cherbourg. They turned west near Sées and came across a French column on the march. After a while Rommel himself went forward to investigate.

'*The French captain declared that Marshal Pétain had made an armistice proposal to Germany and had instructed the French troops to lay down their arms… I then requested the French captain to free the road for our advance and have his column moved off to the fields alongside it and ordered to lay down their arms and fall out. The French captain seemed to hesitate as to whether or not he should do this. Anyway, it took too long to get the French troops into their parking place and so I gave my column orders to move on. We now drove on past the French column, which stood on the road, with its guns and anti-tank guns still limbered up.*'

The 7th Panzer Division drove on into the night and saw, far in front, the pyre of burning supplies at Lessay brightening the sky with its flames. At midnight they entered La-Haye-du-Puits where they saw

'*… a surprising number of men in working clothes standing in the square and behind them a number of lorries laden with material. They were mainly civilian workmen, there were few troops, although several French officers could be seen hurrying busily around. One of them ran through the column directly in front of my car and vanished into a doorway. We drove on… I was just turning over in my mind the detailed deployment of the division in front of Cherbourg, when the head of the column suddenly ran up against a defended*

Carentin, taking advantage of the marshy ground between them, the Marais de Gorges. The five battalions of French Marines were reinforced by the 5th King's Own Scottish Borderers, some anti-tank guns and scout cars and a company of Royal Engineers. This was country the British and the

ABOVE **British troops crowd the desks of the *Guineau* as it pulls away from Cherbourg.**
(IWM F4824)

RIGHT **The British are gone; Cherbourg, June 1940.**
(IWM RML 518)

roadblock and came under very heavy artillery and machine-gun fire.'

Three vehicles went up in flames and, unwilling to put his men at risk, Rommel called a halt. They had, after all, advanced more than 140 miles (225km) that day. Next morning time was spent parleying with the defenders of the roadblock who refused to believe that Pétain had given an order to lay down arms. When Rommel moved in at 8 a.m. to bring the delay to an end the position had been abandoned. On they went, coming under fire a little further on as they made for Barneville. By 12.15 p.m. they were at Les Pieux, some 13 miles (22km) from Cherbourg.

The KOSB had, in the process, been thoroughly outflanked and at 10.15 a.m. Marshall-Cornwall had ordered them to fall back. The Germans were getting too close too fast, and the instructions went out to destroy vehicles. The last of the troops and their commander were on board the SS *Manxman* and putting to sea by 4 p.m. Rommel was, at that moment, congratulating himself on how well things had gone. As soon as the last ship had sailed the French let loose with everything they had got. Rommel reports:

'... a tremendous barrage with guns of all sizes, including super-heavies, into the area which we were holding ... British warships also joined in with heavy naval guns...The positions occupied by the artillery battalion and AA battery came in for particularly heavy attention and casualties soon began to mount.'

He pulled his men back and waited for the rest of his troops to come up. He withdrew to the château at

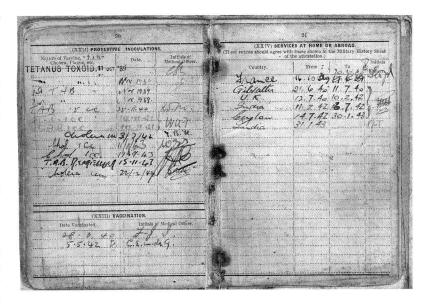

Sotteville which, by chance, was the residence of the commander of Cherbourg and in which they discovered detailed maps of all the fortifications. It became clear to them that the plans now in force were less than perfect; they were changed at once. On Wednesday 19 June Cherbourg fell.

At St Nazaire and at Brest the departure of the British was close to panic-stricken. Assuming that the Germans were hard on their heels, orders were given for personnel only to be embarked and for all vehicles to be destroyed. In Brest the 1st Royal Canadian Horse Artillery protested mightily against the destruction of

ABOVE Gunner Albert Smith's paybook shows the date of his embarkation from France. (Courtesy Albert Smith)

LEFT Hitler and his generals exultant at Compiègne on 21 June. (B122/51624/1)

their guns and, as a result of a series of confusing messages, were already well on the way to completing the loading of their weapons when the order not to do so was confirmed. They lost their vehicles, but not the guns. The last ship sailed on Monday 17 June and the last from St Nazaire the next day. W. Marett of the 1st Ambulance Car Company found himself caught up in the confusion at St Nazaire.

'There were thousands of Frogs there, but our unit bypassed all of them (how or why we never found out) and we boarded a collier. With a full-to-overflowing number of troops aboard we pulled away from the dockside. The German fighters were overhead all the time: it was a very anxious period.

'As we got into more open water, we were suddenly aware that the sea around us was full of British soldiers crying for help. This was a tragic sight but we could do nothing, and the ship kept sailing on. On reaching England we landed at Falmouth, and found out what had happened at St Nazaire. Just ahead of us the liner Lancastria, *a vessel of 20,000 tons with 5,000 men on board, had been bombed and sunk. Upwards of 3,000 men perished.'*

Gunner Albert Smith was still in France. In May, in anticipation of air raids on Italy, the 159 (Lloyds) Battery, 53rd City of London, had been posted to

Salon-de-Provence, about 25 miles (40km) north-west of Marseille. They were taken, by train, in cattle-trucks down the Rhône valley in the warm May sunshine, through the vineyard-clad hills. On arrival they found, to their delight, the cherries were ripe and ready for borrowing. The squadron of Wellington bombers was not there for long, but there the anti-aircraft gunners stayed, apparently forgotten. As the rest of the BEF departed, they were told to get out in any way they could. In Marseille they found the French, unwilling to antagonise the Germans, unhelpful. The dock cranes were switched off and there was no hope of taking their vehicles or guns, so breech blocks were removed and trucks destroyed. Welsh colliers traded with electricity-generating stations in the south of France, and it was on one of these that, on 20 June 1940, Albert Smith and his comrades left for Gibraltar and thence for home. Possibly the last organised embarkation of a full unit from France. One battery of the 53rd City of London Regiment had been on board the *Lancastria*.

The Battle of France was over. On Friday June 21 Adolf Hitler had the satisfaction of seeing the defeated French present themselves at the railway carriage at Compiègne to acknowledge their defeat. It appeared that the triumph was his.

BELOW **The restored Clairière de l'Armistice, dedicated to the victory of 1918 rather than the defeat of 1940.** (MME Hist/Somme 7/9)

BIBLIOGRAPHY

The list that follows includes those books the author has consulted in the course of preparing this work and, in some cases, has quoted from, notably in the cases of the two outstanding German field commanders. The selection is personal and does not pretend to being a comprehensive review of the literature.

Anon., Bomber Command, *The Air Ministry Account of Bomber Command's Offensive Against the Axis, September 1939 – July 1941*, London, HMSO, 1941.

Anon., *Militärgeographische Beschreibung von Frankreich, Teil I, Nordost-Frankreich*, Berlin, Generalstab des Heeres Abteilung für Kriegskarten und Vermessungswesen, 1940.

Baudier, Michel and José Bouchez, *Les Combats de Stonne – Tannay – Oches – Sommauthe du 14 mai au 11 juin 1940*, Fieulaine, l'Association Ardennes 1940, 1997.

Benoist-Méchin, J., trans. Peter Wiles, *Sixty Days that Shook the West*, London, Jonathan Cape, 1963.

Blatt, Joel, (Ed.), *The French Defeat of 1940: Reassessments*, Providence and Oxford, Berghahn, 1998.

Bond, Brian, *Britain, France and Belgium 1939–1940*, 2nd Ed., London, Brasseys, 1990.

Cardigan, the Earl of, *I Walked Alone*, London, Routledge & Keegan Paul, 1950.

Churchill, Winston S., *The Second World War Volume II: Their Finest Hour*, London, Cassell, 1949.

Colville, J. R., *Man of Valour: the Life of Field-Marshal The Viscount Gort*, London, Collins, 1972.

David, Saul, *Churchill's Sacrifice of the Highland Division*, London, Brassey's, 1994.

Deighton, Len, *Blitzkrieg*, London, Jonathan Cape, 1979.

De Gaulle, Charles, trans. Jonathan Griffin, *War Memoirs Volume One, The Call to Honour 1940–1942*, London, Collins, 1955.

Delaforce, Patrick, *Monty's Highlanders*, Brighton, Tom Donovan, 1998.

Divine, A. D., *The Nine Days of Dunkirk*, London, Faber & Faber, 1959.

Doorman, P. L. G., trans. S. L. Salzedo, *Military Operations in the Netherlands from 10th–17th*

May, 1940, London, George Allen & Unwin for the Netherlands Government Information Bureau, 1944.

Ellis, L. F., *The War in France and Flanders 1939–1940*, London, HMSO, 1953; London, Imperial War Museum and Nashville, The Battery Press, 1996.

Fletcher, David, *Mechanised Force: British Tanks between the Wars*, London, HMSO, 1991.

Foss, Christopher F. and Peter McKenzie, *The Vickers Tanks: From Landships to Challenger*, Wellingborough, Patrick Stevens, 1988.

Gander, Terry, 'The explosive attack on Fort Eban-Emael', *Fort Vol. 16*, 1988.

Glover, Michael, *The Fight for the Channel Ports*, London, Leo Cooper, 1985.

Goralski, Robert, *World War II Almanac*, London, Hamish Hamilton, 1981.

Guderian, Heinz, trans. Christopher Duffy, *Achtung – Panzer!*, London, Arms and Armour, 1992.

Guderian, Heinz, trans. Constantine Fitzgibbon, *Panzer Leader*, London, Michael Joseph, 1952.

Harman, Nicholas, *Dunkirk: The Necessary Myth*, London, Hodder and Stoughton, 1980.

Hay, Ian, *The Battle of Flanders 1940*, London, HMSO, 1941.

Holmes, Richard, *Army Battlefield Guide: Belgium and Northern France*, London, HMSO, 1995.

Horne, Alistair, *To Lose a Battle: France 1940*, London, Macmillan, 1969 and 1990.

Horsfall, John, *Say not the Struggle …*, Kineton, The Roundwood Press, 1977.

Jackson, Robert, *Air War over France 1939–40*, London, Ian Allan, 1974.

Jacobsen, Hans-Adolf and Jürgen Rohwer, trans. Edward Fitzgerald, *Decisive Battles of World War II: the German view*, London, André Deutsch, 1965.

Kaufmann, J.E., 'The Dutch and Belgium defences in 1940', *Fort Vol. 17*, 1989.

Keegan, John, (Ed.), *Who's Who in World War II*, London, Weidenfeld & Nicolson, 1978; New York, Oxford University Press, 1995.

Lewin, Ronald, (Ed.), *Freedom's Battle, Volume III: The War On Land 1939–45*, London, Hutchinson, 1969; Pimlico, 1994.

Linklater, Eric, *The Highland Division*, London, HMSO, 1942.

Lord, Walter, *The Miracle of Dunkirk*, New York, Viking, 1982 and London, Allen Lane, 1983; London, Wordsworth, 1998.

Maugham, W. Somerset, *France at War*, London, William Heinemann, 1940.

Maurois, André, trans. F. R. Ludman, *The Battle of France*, London, John Lane The Bodley Head, 1940.

Neave, Airey, *The Flames of Calais*, London, Hodder and Stoughton, 1972.

Pallud, Jean Paul, *Blitzkrieg in the West, Then and Now*, London, Battle of Britain Prints International, 1991.

Perrett, Bryan, and Mike Badrocke, *Panzerkampfwagen III Medium Tank 1936–1944*, Oxford, Osprey Publishing, 1999.

Perrett, Bryan, and Jim Laurier, *Panzerkampfwagen IV 1936–1945*, Oxford, Osprey Publishing, 1999.

Perrett, Bryan, Peter Sarson and Terry Hadler, *German Light Panzers 1932–1942*, Oxford, Osprey Publishing, 1998.

Reitz, Deneys, *No Outspan*, 1943; Prescott, Wolfe Publishing, 1994.

Rommel, Erwin, ed. B.H. Liddell Hart, trans. Paul Findlay, *The Rommel Papers*, London, Collins, 1953.

Seton-Watson, Christopher, *Dunkirk – Alamein – Bologna*, London, Buckland, 1993.

Schulte, Addie, (Ed.), *Oorlogs-reportages uit Nederland & Nederlands Indie: de tweede wereldoorlog in ooggetuigen verslagen*, Amsterdam, Prometheus, 1995.

Snyder, Louis L., *Encyclopedia of the Third Reich*, New York, McGraw-Hill, 1976; London, Wordsworth, 1998.

Sumner, Ian, François Vauvillier and Mike Chappell, *The French Army 1939–1945 (1)*, London, Osprey, 1998.

Time-Life Books, Editors of, *Lightning War*, Alexandria, Time-Life Books, 1989.

Turnbull, Patrick, *Dunkirk: Anatomy of a Disaster*, London, Batsford, 1978.

Ward, Alwyn, *Dunkirk Inspiration*, Sheffield, Alwyn Ward, 1990.

Weinberg, Gerhard L., *A World at Arms*, Cambridge, Cambridge University Press, 1994.

Autumn, 1940. The German grip on France tightens: 'from November 1940 the management of this house is catholic and French, as are the staff. (B146/70/41/56)

INDEX

A wreath laid in memory of the Royal Scots at the CWGC graveyard, Le Paradis. (MME WW2/4/2)